MINISTERS (

The toughest job in government

1945-2018

Brian Edwards (signature)

Professor Brian Edwards

CONTENTS

Chapter 1　　　Ministers and the NHS

Chapter 2　　　The individual ministers

Chapter 3　　　What makes a good Minister of Health ?

Appendix 1　　Details about individual ministers

Professor Brian Edwards is Emeritus Professor of Health Care Development at the University of Sheffield where he was Dean of the School of Health and Related Research. Prior to this he had an extended career as a Chief Executive in the NHS which entailed a close engagement with ministers and civil servants at the Department of Health. He is an honorary doctor of medicine. He has lectured and published widely in the field of health policy and for three years was President of the European Hospital Federation.

Ministers and the NHS

1946-2018

The Secretary of State for Health is one of the most challenging and arduous political posts in modern government. It has never been on the political route map to Downing Street for ambitious politicians. Despite this many of its holders have come to regard their time in office as the most rewarding of their political careers. This book looks first at the common policy themes they faced and then at each of the post holders and describes what happened during their tenure and what they achieved. Finally, I offer a judgement as to what makes a good Secretary of State for Health.

There have been twenty-nine Ministers of the NHS in the period between 1946 and 2018.[1] The term NHS has never actually been included in the ministerial title but its future and day to day problems have nevertheless dominated the time and energy of every Minister of Health. In Bevan's day the ministerial brief included Housing, but this was lost when he moved on. For twenty years from 1968 the brief explicitly included social security and the Ministry was called the DHSS [Department of Health and Social Security]. For some ministers like Crossman social security was a major preoccupation. It is from Crossman's time that the term Secretary of State is applied to the lead politician. A junior member of the ministerial team usually had social security in their title and this

---

[1] There were Ministries of Health from 1919, but without an NHS.

included John Major the future Prime Minister. In 1988 Margaret Thatcher broke up the DHSS into two ministries one named the Department of Health under Kenneth Clarke and the other the Department of Social Security under John Moore. Social security later became part of the Department of Work and Pensions. Planning for the future of social care returned to the Ministry of Health in 2018 under Jeremy Hunt.

The average age of a Minister of Health or Secretary of State on appointment since 1945 is 50 years. Iain Macleod [1952] and Andy Burnham [2009] have been the youngest at 39 years of age and Richard Crossman [61] and Barbara Castle [64] were the oldest. There have only been three women; Barbara Castle, Virginia Bottomley and Patricia Hewitt.

Many of the early ministers had served in the armed forces, often with distinction. Six had been called to the Bar prior to entering Parliament.[2] Seven could be described as having strong roots in the trade union movement.[3] Just over half were educated at Oxford or Cambridge and many held a leading position in university student associations. None have been a registered health professional. There have been three doctors, one nurse and one Director of Social Services amongst the ranks of junior health ministers.[4]

The only ministers with any significant connection with health policy prior to their appointment were Ennals, Clarke, Bottomley, Milburn and Burnham all of whom had worked as a Minister of State in Health, the number two position under the Secretary of State.[5] Few can claim to have any experience of managing large complex organisations.

Seventeen ministers came from the Conservative Party and twelve from Labour. Conservatives have had a longer spell in control of the NHS by some fifteen years. The average period in office averages out at just over two and a half years. Four served for a year or less. Only three Bevan, Fowler and Hunt served for longer than five years in the top post.

| J Hunt | Conservative | 5 years 309 days |

---

[2] Turton, Walker-Smith, Barber, Joseph, Jenkin and Clarke.
[3] Bevan, Castle, Dobson, Milburn, Reid, Hewitt and Johnson.
[4] Owen, Trafford, Vaughan, Milton [PUS], Warner
[5] Andy Burnham worked for the NHS Confederation prior to his election as an MP.

N Fowler	Conservative	5 years 273 days
A Bevan	Labour	5 years 167 days
K Robinson	Labour	4 years 14 days
K Joseph	Conservative	3 years 258 days
A Milburn	Labour	3 years 245 days
I McLeod	Conservative	3 years 227 days
V Bottomley	Conservative	3 years 86 days
E Powell	Conservative	3 years 85 days
D Ennals	Labour	3 years 27 days

Each Secretary of State was confronted with different challenges on taking office, but some policy questions were common to all. Cash for the NHS has always been an issue and to varying degrees all got involved with the annual negotiations with the Treasury. Their reputation both within the NHS and with the wider public was to some extent influenced by their success in securing a good settlement. Only three managed to negotiate major increases in investment. Enoch Powell won a major capital injection to fund his hospital rebuilding programme in the early 1960s. Alan Milburn secured an agreement with Tony Blair and Gordon Brown to match the European average spend[6] and fund his NHS Plan in 2000 [although the credit for this must be shared with Frank Dobson his predecessor]. Jeremy Hunt secured a major cash injection towards the end of his term in office in 2018 but only after a long period of austerity and a prolonged cap on public sector pay rises. As the years went by the negotiations with the Treasury became more heated and more sophisticated. An aging population, an expanding science base and growing public expectation made for lots of argument. By 2010 NHS expenditure had reached 7.59 % of GDP. It then fell back during the years of austerity to a forecast 7.07 in 2019/20.

Experts claim that the NHS needs an annual growth rate of around 4% to keep up with the needs of an aging population and advances in clinical science. This has rarely been achieved. Instead ministers have usually demanded greater efficiency within the NHS claiming any savings can be reinvested to fund new services. Fowler introduced a powerful performance review system and ordered the competitive tendering of contracts for housekeeping services. The

---

[6] In 2000 the UK share of GDP was 7. France was 10.1 and Germany 10.4

internal market created by Thatcher and Clarke in 1991 was founded on the believe that competition would improve performance, quality and responsiveness to patients. Thatcher was much engaged by evidence about wide and in her view unjustified variations in lengths of hospital stay for procedures such as cataract removal. In practice the public usually saw the market as a means of cost cutting and privatisation. As Duncan Nichol, the first Chief Executive to come from within the NHS put it "we spent too much time explaining what a market was rather than why it was necessary and what it might achieve ", A similar criticism would be made some years later about the Lansley reforms. Badly presented reforms rarely succeed.

The NHS has always been close to the centre of political debate in the UK. It has often been a major issue in general elections. The politics of the NHS can be savage and brutal. It is an easy target for politicians in opposition and it has proved exceedingly difficult to ever secure a wide political consensus on changes. As Rudolf Klein put it" as an institution the NHS has ranked next to the monarchy in the political landscape of Britain". Nigel Lawson, a former Chancellor, put it thus" The NHS is the closest thing the English people have now to a religion". The NHS is firmly embedded in the identity of Great Britain.

The Conservatives have always been accused by the Labour party of attempting to privatise the NHS either by replacing Treasury funding with health insurance or by allowing private providers of care to treat NHS patients. Many Tory prime ministers have denied this including Margaret Thatcher "The NHS is safe with us" and John Major "There will be no privatisation of health care whilst I am Prime Minister"[7].

Labour ministers, who regard the NHS as something they created, want it to remain in the public sector but have on occasion used the private sector to reduce NHS waiting lists. It is important in this argument to distinguish between competition and privatisation. The NHS could retain its principles and secure services to the community free to all at the point of need if it operated simply as an insurer, but this has proved too difficult an argument to win. Frank Dobson [Labour] promised to demolish the internal market, but Alan Milburn [Labour] left most of it in place. He accepted that there was a place for

---

[7] John Major. The Autobiography

a regulated private sector in modern health care[8]. In 2018 the NHS spent about 11% of its budget in the private sector.[9] A new front in this battle may be developing as private providers move into the primary care field deploying web-based services.

The persistent demands from the Treasury for increased efficiency led them to develop a much-criticised efficiency index for the NHS in the 1980s. The index was very focused on the acute sector of medicine to the detriment, some claimed, of the Cinderella services. In his time Hunt had to accept wholly unachievable efficiency targets to secure even a modicum of growth. The Ministry of Health has a good record of balancing its overall budget but during periods of stress ministers have not hesitated to intervene directly. In 1953 MacLeod introduced a national manpower freeze on the NHS. No medical consultant post anywhere in the country could be filled without Ministry approval. Fowler introduced national controls over manpower numbers. Clarke and others imposed strict limits on management costs. Labour ministers followed Frank Dobson's example and sent in hit squads to sort out failing NHS organisations. Patricia Hewitt sacked Nigel Crisp the NHS Chief Executive because of his handling of rampant overspending in some parts of the NHS. Labour MPs were angry at his public warning that some Primary Care Trusts would have to start divesting themselves of some of the services they were operating.

Barbara Castle and David Ennals her successor took steps to equalise investment across England [10]which caused years of strain in London but allowed new hospitals to be built in the midlands and the north. Other ministers have sought to switch the balance of investment between the acute sector and the so-called *Cinderella* services. In the long term the glamour and higher profile of acute medicine has usually prevailed. The specific, and huge, investment in mental health in 2018 may turn out to be an exception to this rule.

Capital investment has always been a problem and has always been accounted for separately from revenue. The NHS inherited an ancient estate. The sale of

---

[8] Rejuvenate or retire. Views of the NHS at 60.
[9] John Appleby. Nuffield Trust.
[10] Similar equalisation policies were adopted in the rest of the United Kingdom.

land and buildings on the closure of the Asylum system helped but only after ministers agreed to leave the sales income in the regions where it had been generated for local reinvestment. Enoch Powell's Hospital plan saw the building of many new District General Hospitals, which proved expensive to run and created more demand in the system. The new breed of hospital consultant wanted to deploy their skills and patients wanted to benefit from their care. This was the time when new clinical sciences and clinical specialisation began to expand.

A crucial piece of economic theory came into play as the NHS expanded in the 1960's. Beveridge had argued that as society became fitter and heathier the demands on the NHS would fall. Enoch Powell challenged this theory by describing the infinity of demand for health care. The Milburn investment in 2000 which sharply reduced waiting lists and created new services certainly proved to be inflationary and Patricia Hewitt inherited the storm that followed. Hunt accepted the case for putting the whole of the NHS on a full 24/7 basis. He thought it would save lives despite the lack of any compelling evidence that it would have this result. It was an extremely expensive decision and soaked up much of the additional manpower that had been injected in the system. Personalised care for the elderly is undoubtably good but it has largely failed to take the pressure off the hospital sector. Instead it has exposed unmet demand in the community.

Cash for the NHS has never been far from the top of any minister's in-tray.

Any significant changes to the NHS have usually ended up with a political row. The British Medical Association fought hard to stop Bevan creating the NHS but since its formation have fought almost all politically inspired change and presented themselves as its great defender. Some ministers like Kenneth Robinson were highly respected by the BMA which led to allegations from colleagues in government that he was in their pocket. Iain Macleod was hailed as a true friend of doctors by the then President of the Royal College of Surgeons. Although the BMA was sad to see Powell go, he commented in his memoirs that "The unnerving discovery every minister of health makes at or near the outset of his term of office is that the only subject he is destined to discuss with the medical profession is money". Castle and her medically trained deputy Owen had a furious argument with the BMA about pay beds.

Clarke had a serious fight about the introduction of the internal market. He too used a memorable phase at one of the professions grand dinners "I do wish the more suspicious of our GPs would stop feeling nervously for their wallets every time I mention the word reform. "He knew as did most managers that the way to get change in primary care had always been via the GP payments system. Milburn on taking office told the BMA that they were in the last chance saloon. Change or die he said.

Junior doctors and their hours of work have often been a problem. Some wanted their hours reduced whilst others wanted their long hours better rewarded. The Royal College of Surgeons argued that long hours were essential to develop skills. A settlement of sorts was finally negotiated by Jeremy Hunt.

Trade Unions representing other groups of staff have also caused problems from time to time. The ancillary staff unions broke through the emotional barrier against strike action in the NHS in the 1970s and others followed including nurses. Pay has always been a national issue despite numerous attempts to devolve it to NHS field authorities. The creation of so-called independent pay review bodies was often ministers way of defusing issues [although they did not always accept this independent advice]. A new pay structure in 2004 [Agenda for Change] simplified pay structures and has stood the test of time.

Local change has also proved problematic when it involved closing local hospitals or moving specialist services. London was particularly resistant to change. Small community hospitals have been closed by some ministers and saved by others.

Engaging local communities in the day to day affairs of their local NHS has been a target for some ministers. Leagues of Hospital friends are not as prominent as they were in the early years. Medical charities now operate largely on a national basis. Community Health Councils were formed in 1974 with the power to refer planned local changes to a minister if they disagreed with them. They were abolished in 2000. They had become very politicised and objected to almost all change. As one ex minister put it "they became oppositionists " [11] Other mechanisms have followed but none has been very

---

[11] Gisela Stuart.

effective. Personal health budgets which have been promoted by both parties may be more effective in generating patient sensitivity. They do not however fit comfortably with a cash limited service focused on priority setting for whole communities.

Modern political parties regularly sound out public opinion. The NHS has always scored highly. A Kings Fund/Mori study in 2017 found that 90% of people support the founding principles of the NHS. There is unwavering support amongst the public which has endured across generations. This explains why no party in power has ever seriously challenged these principles. A service free to all based on clinical need and funded primarily from general taxation is deeply embedded in British Society. A modest decision to introduce prescription charges in the early years provoked the resignation of Bevan. A Royal Commission set by Harold Wilson to review the funding and management of the NHS confirmed the value of an NHS as did numerous later commissions. The Wanless reports commissioned by Gordon Brown confirmed that general taxation was the most efficient way of funding the NHS although to the shock of Gordon Brown he reported that in some areas of medicine the UK results were amongst the worst in Europe. Even radical reformers like Margaret Thatcher have declined to challenge the principle. She firmly rejected plans developed by one of her policy think tanks to move to a system of health insurance. In modern times the question has shifted to whether or not the public will pay to sustain a modern system that keeps abreast of new technology. Medicine is becoming increasingly expensive and costs are forecast to increase sharply as personalised medicine based on the DNA profile of individual patients develops. The health share of GDP will need to significantly increase to keep up with medical science.

One exception to high approval ratings has been the time patients must wait for non-emergency surgery and diagnostic tests. A number of ministers have sought to get waiting times reduced. Some like Bottomley provided earmarked national funds which worked. The Patients Charter launched by John Major set targets which were increasingly met and waiting times fell. Labour ministers like Milburn encouraged the use of private hospitals to treat NHS patients and again waiting times reduced. By 2018, 500,00 NHS patients were being treated in private hospitals. In the years of austerity under Hunt the targets were dropped and the waiting lists grew again to near record levels. The public strongly supported the waiting time reductions, but the BMA objected. Decisions to treat were they argued now being made according to patients place in the queue rather than clinical priority.

From the start of the NHS Bevan had promised the medical profession clinical freedom. Government would not interfere, he promised, in decisions about individual patients. This concordat held by and large for the first forty years. But from the 1980's it began to contract and fade. The reasons are complicated, but they include the emergence of multidisciplinary treatment programmes, clinical audit and a closer oversight of individual professionals. By the 1980's medicine had become increasingly complex and specialised. No longer could a single doctor possess all the knowledge and skills to treat all his patients. Vaccination and immunisation had largely conquered common childhood disease, joint replacement was becoming commonplace as was organ transplantation. Both quickly grew waiting lists. Lengths of stay in hospital began to reduce with improved anaesthetic and surgical technique as did the development of day surgery. Psychiatry finally had drugs to treat their patients. Medicine was on the move at a quickening pace which has accelerated again in modern times. Cancer is now treatable. The NHS is increasingly focused on the health needs of the elderly. Gene therapy and personalised medicine may be the next great leaps forward.

The other event that forced government closer to clinical practice was targets based on judgements about the health of the nation. The plan was published by William Waldegrave in 1992. There were targets for reductions in coronary heart disease, breast cancer, suicide and others. One target was smoking reduction which had had a very chequered history inside the Ministry with early ministers denying both any causation between smoking and cancer and their responsibility to intervene. As rationing became the alternative way of describing choices in a cash limited system, ministers like Dorrell resisted total bans on some clinical procedures such as tattoo or adenoid removal. Frank Dobson, who had intervened to limit the availability of Viagra on the NHS, was later to create NICE to decide which treatments and drugs could be made available to NHS patients on a cost-effective basis. The other public health issue that ministers got heavily involved in was Aids. Norman Fowler led a very controversial campaign to educate the public about the dangers of certain sexual behaviour and forced the pace in the search for effective treatments.

General practice has presented problems for ministers from time to time. Robinson with his GP Charter resurrected it in the 1960s with cash for premises and the attachment of community nursing and midwifery staff to practices. In 2003 Alan Milburn allowed GPs to withdraw from a requirement to be available twenty fours a day for their patients. In recent years the burden of looking after an aging population has been instrumental in persuading an increasing number of doctors to opt for a salary rather than a share in a practice. Many now work part-time for the NHS.

GP Fundholding switched somewhat the balance of power between GPs and hospital consultants and GP's lead role in commissioning NHS services has continued with the support of both parties. Politicians have discovered that doctors can ration services easier than they can.

For the first 25 years the NHS had a stable administrative structure. It all changed in 1974 with the creation of Heath Authorities that encompassed both primary and secondary care. As a policy, integration met little resistance but the finely detailed management structure that was imposed on the whole system quickly broke down leading to more reorganisations. Ministers and their civil servants believed in the power of reorganisation to deliver their view of a future NHS. On almost every occasion they promised major financial savings which never materialised. It did however give the illusion of progress. One policy that has survived since the Clarke era and through successive changes in government has been that of giving hospitals their operational freedoms as NHS Trusts. It was Gordon Brown who limited their financial freedoms.

Ideas about an independent NHS Board had been around even before the Royal Commission recommended against it in 1979. Norman Fowler was however more sympathetic to the idea. He recruited a man from industry, Victor Paige to manage the NHS from within the Department of Health. Although he wanted somebody to run the NHS, he made it clear he was still in charge. "Officials advice, ministers decide" he explained. These early developments led eventually to creation of the NHS Executive based in Leeds.

For the next 15 years it managed the NHS under quite close ministerial oversight and occasional interference. In 1986 Bottomley got rid of NHS regions partly to clear the ground for the NHS Executive. It was Milburn who closed the NHS Executive down in 2001 claiming that its independence was a fiction. Ideas about an independent organisation remerged under Lansley and NHS England was created to oversee the commissioning arm of the NHS. Hospitals and other providers would have the freedoms that came from foundation status.

The NHS needs competent and skilled management. Ministers cannot run the NHS from Whitehall. There has never been any real doubt that ministers are accountable to Parliament for the NHS although none has ever resigned because of its mistakes or shortcomings. Many heads have rolled within the NHS. Lansley wanted to stop ministers meddling in NHS operational matters, but Parliament demanded that he remained ultimately accountable. This will remain the case whilst ever the government is the principle paymaster

The balance between a national service and local management has been a constant tension within the Ministry. Bevan won the argument with Herbert Morrison about an NHS separate from Local Government but many of his predecessors sought to bring the two closer together. Some added local councillors to health boards, others provided ring fenced funds to stimulate collaboration. Health and Wellbeing Boards are the latest attempt to coordinate health and local authority planning and operations. Labour politicians used the post code lottery as an attack weapon. It did highlight geographical variations within the system but did nothing to encourage local decision making and priority setting.

Luck has sometimes influenced ministerial careers when well worked up policies initiated by their predecessors were presented to them by their permanent secretaries on appointment. This is true of Enoch Powell with the Hospital Plan the groundwork for which had been initiated by Walker- Smith. The same might be said of Bevan who inherited a political consensus to create an NHS and a well worked up plan for him to change, mould and shape. Having developed his plan Bevan then fought it through Parliament in the teeth of strong opposition. Ennals implemented Barbara Castle's plan to equalise investment across the English regions[12]. Virginia Bottomley took charge of Waldegrave's Health of the Nation policies.

Bad luck has also played its part as politicians entered the Ministry only to face a full-blown crisis or major scandal that was none of their making. This was true of Patricia Hewitt. Some ministers had assumed office with well-formed plans of their own. Clarke, Dobson, Milburn and Lansley fall into this group. Others like Hunt grew into the job. A few like Robinson, Ennals and Bottomley displayed an emotional commitment to health that played out well with the health professions.

Quality took centre stage in the wake of the inquiries into poor care at Mid Staffordshire Hospitals which it was alleged had led to many deaths. Robert Francis the Inquiry chair blamed the culture of the NHS with its focus on financial control, top down targets and an insensitivity to patient voices. Andy Burnham came under a lot of pressure during this Inquiry. Hunt's reaction was to tell managers that quality and safety were more important than financial control. The inevitable consequence was a burgeoning debt.

Most Secretaries of State had a plan of some sort which stretched well beyond their term of office. Trouble was, they wanted, as Dobson rather inelegantly put it "instant gratification". New plans were of course more important than those of a predecessor. It kept the policy teams busy, but the NHS confused about priorities. Sometimes a new Secretary of State stimulated more policy shifts than a change of government.

One should never understate the burden of office with its incessant pressure and problems that come out of the blue. The role requires physical and emotional strength. Vosper, Ennals and Moore where never in the best of health. Milburn was said to be exhausted at the end of his term in office.

Within the Ministry ministers found plenty of advice and personal support. A modern team comprises six politicians. Each minister has a private office who act as the focus for officials reporting in on matters affecting a ministers' areas of responsibility. Each minister has their own detailed list which can range from information technology to psychiatry. Alan Johnson took a small team

---

[12] Similar equalisation policies were adopted in the rest of the UK.

with him as moved around various ministries in Whitehall. Relationships between ministers and the civil service have varied over years. Some permanent secretaries worked very closely with their Secretaries of State. Stowe and Fowler were together for nearly six years. Others found their political masters more challenging. Chris Kelly and Alan Milburn never made it work. The best Secretaries of State used their civil service support very effectively and drew them into a partnership.

The Secretary of State for Health and Social Welfare is undoubtably one of the toughest and most complex jobs in government today.

Aneurin Bevan

August 1945- January 1951

Labour

Nye Bevan had his roots in the coal fields of South Wales where he was a miner and a trade union activist. In 1919 he secured a scholarship to the Central Labour College in London where his left-wing socialist views were consolidated. In the general strike in 1926 he emerged as one of the leaders of the South Wales miners with a reputation as a fiery orator. He entered Parliament in 1929 as MP for Ebbw Vale a seat he held until his death. He was a constant critic of Winston Churchill during the Second World War. Churchill called him a squalid nuisance. Bevan described the Conservatives as vermin. After Dunkirk he called for the impeachment of those who were responsible, including Chamberlain. He was a stormy petrel with a magic all his own and is described by Kenneth Morgan a Welsh historian as "the most hated-if also the most idolised-politician of his time". He had a reputation for making the smooth, rough and elevating the most trivial disputes into matters of serious controversy.[13] He was expelled from the Labour Party for a brief period in 1939 along with Stafford Cripps for platform sharing with groups like the communists in pursuit of creating a popular front against fascism.

The debate about health service reform had been underway throughout the war following the Beveridge Report in 1942. Two separate White papers had been published in 1943 and 1944 after protracted negotiations with all the interested parties. The Treasury were very sceptical about a free NHS.

The Labour Party manifesto for the 1945 election included a promise to make the best health services available free to all. Money, it said, must no longer be the passport to the best treatment.

It was a surprise to many when Clement Attlee appointed Bevan to the post of Minister of Health [which at that time included Housing another major social priority after the war]. He was the youngest member of Attlee's cabinet and it was to be his first and only major ministerial appointment.[14]

When he came into office William Douglas the Permanent Secretary presented Bevan with a plan for health reform that had been worked up with his predecessor Henry Willink. It committed the government to a comprehensive health service, free to all and a service that would promote good health. This plan protected the independence of the voluntary hospitals but required them to operate and develop within the plans drawn up by Regional and Area Planning Boards. Local Authorities would keep control of services that they were running including municipal hospitals. General Practitioners would retain their independence.

Bevan, whilst fully committed to the principle of a national health service, did not like this plan at all which he thought was a "hopelessly impractical compromise based not upon functional considerations but merely upon a desire to conciliate conflicting interests".[15] Others agreed with him including some civil servants who thought the plan to be of unworkable complexity.[16] Bevan quickly developed an alternative plan for tripartite administration [Local

---

[13] Bevan. Clare Beckett and Francis Beckett. Haus Publishing 2004.
[14] His move to the Ministry of Labour in January 1951 was short lived as he resigned after only three months in protest at the introduction of prescription charges.
[15] Willink did not like this at all and objected during a debate on the second reading of the NHS Bill to the "actions of a Minister of Health who has overthrown the judgement of those so far more experienced".
[16] John E Pater. The making of the NHS. Kings Fund. London 1981.

Authorities, Executive Councils and Hospital Management Committees] and most radical of all a plan to nationalise and regionalise the whole of the hospital sector including both Voluntary and Municipal hospitals. The new service was to be nationally funded and free to all citizens at the point of need. He resisted pressure in Cabinet from Herbert Morrison who wanted the new NHS to be firmly rooted in local government.

Bevan published his own White Paper and then Bill;

[1] *It shall be the duty of the Minister of Health to promote the establishment…. of a comprehensive health service designed to secure improvement in the physical and mental health of the people and the prevention, diagnosis and treatment of illness;*

[2] *The services so provided shall be free of charge.*

He steered the Bill through Parliament in the teeth of major opposition from the BMA and others. The BMA complained bitterly that the changes would turn doctors from free thinking professionals into salaried servants of the State. Bevan countered this by accepting the principles of clinical freedom. "It will be a basic principle of the new service that there should be no interference with the clinical freedom of any doctor-specialist or general practitioner".[17]

In general practice the payment structure was a major issue as was the selling of practices which Bevan regarded as evil. Patients themselves should decide which practice to register with and not find themselves sold on to another doctor. In the end the compromise for general practice was self-employed independent practitioner status and a capitation fee related to the number of patients on a doctors list. The sale of practices was banned, and it was hoped that many doctors would practice from health centres.

With the Consultants he agreed a basic national salary with the right to treat private patients in NHS hospitals and a merit awards scheme operated by the medical profession to stimulate and reward the best clinical practice.[18] Consultant medical staff would be employed at a regional level except for

---

[17] Aneurin Bevan. Michael Foot.1973
[18] Depending on the scale of private practice Consultants might have to accept a one eleventh reduction in NHS pay.

those in teaching hospitals who would be appointed by their local Board of Governors. He had, he later said, stuffed the Consultants mouths with gold.

The Voluntary Hospitals resisted Bevan at first but eventually worked out that they would be better in a regionalised system than being municipalised. In any case many were insolvent.

It was a bold and radical plan.

On the 5th April 1948, 1143 Voluntary Hospitals and 1545 Municipal Hospitals in the United Kingdom were taken over by the NHS. General Practice remained independent but was supervised and paid by 38 Executive Councils whose membership was dominated by the health professions. Local authorities continued to run district nursing and maternal and child welfare services but their role in health was sharply diminished. Access to the NHS was free to all at the point of need. Within a few months 97% of the British public signed up along with 90% of general practitioners.

Bevan insisted that the Ministers in charge of the NHS be clearly accountable to Parliament. He wanted "the sound of a bed pan dropped in Tredegar to reverberate around the Palace of Westminster" or in another version "The Minister of Health will be the whipping boy for the National Health Service in Parliament; every time a maid kicks over a bucket of slops in a ward an agonised wail will go through Whitehall."[19] He recognised the tension between ministerial accountability and devolved management to non-elected bodies which was to confront many of his predecessors. Regional Hospital Boards, he said, had to have a vitality of their own but "it is still difficult to envisage a situation which in order to give to them vitality they were left free to spend exchequer money without ministerial approval. His solution was to make Regional Hospital Boards accountable to the Ministry of Health and make them operate under broad financial and ministerial control. Almost from day one the NHS overspent its allocation and Bevan had to fight hard in Cabinet for extra funding. He strongly resisted any ideas about the introduction of NHS charges. In 1950/51 charges were avoided and the budget ceiling was increased to £392m in exchange for Bevan agreeing to a Cabinet Committee chaired by the Prime Minister to monitor NHS expenditure.[20][21]

---

[19] This version from Foot was part of a speech to the Institute of Almoners in March 1946.

Bevan understood that his NHS contained several uncomfortable compromises that would have to be dealt with by his successors. In rejecting calls for a salaried general practice, he explained that "there is all the difference in the world between plucking fruit when it is ripe and plucking it when it is green". It would take fifty years for salaried GPs to operate in the NHS. Had he stayed in office longer his next target would probably have been modernising general practice which was, he was advised, in a bad state and getting worse.

In housing he produced a major expansion of the national house building programme. He was determined to see the end of city ghettos.

In 1951 having secured an agreement from Stafford Cripps, the Chancellor of the Exchequer, that the NHS would remain charge free, Bevan moved to the post of Minister for Labour. He resigned after only 3 months in protest at the introduction of prescription charges in the NHS by Hugh Gaitskell who had been appointed Chancellor of the Exchequer. Bevan had made it plain to colleagues that he would not serve as a member of a government that levied charges on patients in order to rearm for a Korean war. Harold Wilson, a future prime minister, resigned with him.[22] The sum involved was only £13m but as Bevan put it "what will he do next year?"

Labour lost the 1951 general election and Bevan went into opposition and acted as the leader of the left wing of the Labour Party [The Bevanites]. In 1952 he published "In Place of Fear"[23] setting out his political philosophy. In 1959 he became deputy leader of the Labour Party until he died in 1960. In many ways it was inside the Party that he had his fiercest rows and where he generated a deal of rancour. He was expelled from the Labour party for a brief period in 1939.

He was liked and admired by his civil servants for his passion and his energy although they were at first resistant to his ideas about the structure of the NHS preferring instead the Willink plan. He often walked around the Ministry talking to junior staff with the tacit approval of William Douglas the Permanent Secretary. Douglas thought Bevan to be the best Minister he had ever worked

---

[20] Stafford Cripps. Simon Burgess.1999. Gollancz.
[21] In 1951 NHS expenditure amounted to 3.4% of GDP.
[22] Wilson had worked as a research assistant to William Beveridge during the war.
[23] In Place of Fear. Heineman. London.1952

for. Hugh Dalton the Chancellor of the Exchequer between 1945-47 was a strong supporter and Bevan was often a visitor at 11 Downing Street. Dalton played a major role in helping Bevan get the NHS off the ground.[24] Bevan was a good tactician in Parliament and at times, but not always, a great orator. At the time of his resignation speech according to one colleague "he bawled and, in that Welsh voice almost screamed." His scathing logic was often deployed against his opponents.[25] He handled the Tory lawyers with a "scintillating and dialectical brilliance "said one of his colleagues Sir Frederick Messer. His true genius according to Henry Fairlie was "as the perpetual enemy of the complacency that affects free and apparently affluent societies."[26] Even the BMA recognised his qualities with one of its leaders telling colleagues "Mr Bevan is a charming and brilliant man, strongly convinced about the ends he has in view, though not careful enough of the means whereby he gains them. He is no village tyrant, but a big man on a big errand. If the profession is to stand in his way, as I hope it will, it means a very grave decision."[27]

He will always be remembered as the man who created the NHS.

[1897-1960]

HILARY MARQUAND

1951 [January-October]

Labour

Hilary Marquand was born and educated in Cardiff. An academic by background he had been appointed Professor of Industrial Relations at University College, Cardiff in 1930 at the age of 29. This made him, at the time, the youngest professor in a British University. He played a major role in diagnosing the economic ills of South Wales and was involved in the preparation of several plans for economic recovery. In 1945 he was elected as

---

[24] Hugh Dalton. Ben Pimlott. Macmillan 1985.
[25] Herbert Morrison. Donoghue and Jones .1973
[26] Eminent Parliamentarians. The Speakers Lectures 2012.Biteback publishing. London
[27] Aneurin Bevan. Michael Foot

a Labour MP for Cardiff East. In 1950 he fought and won the seat in Middlesbrough which he held until his retirement in 1961.He had spent his war years in various ministries culminating as Labour Advisor to the Ministry of Production. After the Labour victory in 1945 he became Secretary for Overseas Trade, Paymaster General and Minister for Pensions.

In 1951 Clement Attlee asked him to take over from Aneurin Bevan at the Ministry of Health. The post had lost its housing responsibilities as well as its seat in the cabinet. He spent much of his time tidying up the consequences of creating an NHS. Tuberculosis and hearing aids were a regular focus for parliamentary questions as was the planned reorganisation of the hospitals in Kingston upon Thames. Stafford Cripps, the Chancellor of the Exchequer, had enforced a £400m ceiling on NHS expenditure. He was only in post for nine months because of the Conservative election victory in October 1951.He was regarded as a humane and able administrator, but he might have been better placed in the Foreign and Commonwealth Office where his interests and expertise lay.

He resigned his seat in Parliament in 1961 to take up the post as Director of the International Institute for Labour Studies in Geneva.

[1901-1972.]

HARRY CROOKSHANK

October1951-May 1952

Conservative

Harry Crookshank was born in Egypt the son of a surgeon who was also the Director General of the Egyptian Prison Administration.[28] After his father's death the family returned to London. After Eton Crookshank went on to Oxford and on completing his studies joined the Grenadier Guards at the start of the first world war. He was seriously injured and castrated by shrapnel in 1916.

---

[28] Oxford Dictionary of National Biography

After the war Captain Crookshank joined the Diplomatic Service and in 1921 was posted to the High Commission in Constantinople.

He was elected MP for Gainsborough in Lincolnshire in 1924 and became a Commons character. He had a reputation as a natty dresser and a man who had quixotic affairs.[29] His first ministerial post came in 1934 when he was appointed Minister for Mines. He did not get on well with Winston Churchill. He entered the Cabinet in 1951 as Minister for Health a post that was combined with the deputy Leader of the House of Commons.

His short tenure as a Minister in Health was dominated by austerity and this is reflected in his answers to parliamentary questions which were usually short and factual. Shortages of cortisone and X-Ray film, cuts in the NHS capital programme, cheese rations and the size of Regional Hospital Boards dominated his questions.

He failed to persuade cabinet colleagues to introduce hotel charges for patients, but they did agree to his proposals for charges for medicines and dental treatment[30]. He was also very influential in securing cabinet agreement to the Danckwerts Report which recommended big increases for general practitioners. He was an experienced minister who knew the corners as well as the corridors of power.[31] When Parliament was sitting it took precedence and soaked up most of his time. He chaired several cabinet committees [including the Steel Committee] and was the principle arbiter of the government's legislative programme. He was a very busy Parliamentarian.

His period in Health was not judged to be a great success but by all accounts, his officials liked and respected his intellect and his zeal. He was particularly interested in mental health. In 1952 he accepted a sinecure post of Lord Privy seal which left him time to concentrate on his role as Leader of the Commons. He led a walkout of ministers in 1954 in response to Churchill's decision to build a British H bomb after consultation with only selected ministers. Eden sacked him as Leader of the House in 1955 and he moved to the House of Lords as Viscount Crookshank. He established the Crookshank lecture at the

---

[29] Oxford Dictionary of National Biography
[30] One shilling prescription charge; one-pound dental treatment and part payment for surgical body and abdominal supports, wigs and hosiery.
[31] Iain Macleod. Nigel Fisher. 1973. Andre Deutch.

Royal College of Radiology in his sister's memory. His funeral took place in Westminster Abbey and he is buried at Lincoln Cathedral,

[1893-1961]

IAIN MACLEOD

May 1952- December 1955

Conservative

Iain Macleod was born in Yorkshire. His father was a General Practitioner. He read History at Cambridge before embarking on a career as a bridge player. He won the Gold Cup in 1937.He suffered a serious war injury in France in 1940 which was to cause discomfort for the rest of his life.[32] He returned to France on D Day and ended the war as a Major. He joined what became the Conservative Party Research Department in 1946 before he entered Parliament in 1950 as MP for Enfield West. A brilliant Commons performance against Aneurin Bevan on health caught the attention of Winston Churchill then Prime Minister.[33] Six weeks later he was appointed Minister of Health. It was not at this time a cabinet post. It was his first ministerial appointment and he shares with Andy Burnham[34] the designation as the youngest ever appointed at 39 years. Sir John Hawton the Permanent Secretary at the time found him initially to be diffident, modest and unsure of himself. This assessment was to change radically as Macleod's confidence grew. Civil servants grew to be impressed with his clear thinking and attentive memory.

---

[32] His wife Eve was disabled with polio in 1952 during his term of office. After his death she accepted a seat in the Lords.
[33] He and Bevan were parliamentary "pairs" and enjoyed a good relationship.
[34] 2009-2010

He always read his briefs. Others describe him as charismatic, cerebral and socially liberal.[35] George Godber the CMO, who became a close friend, liked his ability to handle awkward deputations without notes in front of him. He had a reputation as a great orator and raconteur with a sonorous voice.

In one of his early meetings with senior civil servants he told them that he wanted the NHS to enjoy a period of tranquillity, with no drastic reorganisations.[36] An early challenge was the consequences of the great smog in December 1952 which caused over 4000 deaths and led to the Clean Air Act in 1956. Throughout Macleod's period of office funds were tight and one of his early acts was to prune regional capital programmes. He believed that the size of the overall social services budget should be related to the good it did which must outweigh the burden it placed on individuals and industry. His term was a period of consolidation and he left the NHS much as he found it. He told Bevan that he did not find the need to radically change his vision. He did however want to redevelop the link between the State and local communities. Every hospital he said should have its own League of Friends and this applied particularly to hospitals for the mentally ill. "I know", he said," when I go into a hospital whether it has a League of Friends or not-there is a different atmosphere ". In 1954 he doubled the capital investment in mental health at the expense of other parts of the NHS. He also told hospitals to allow parents to visit their children in hospital every day instead of once a week. He supported health charges arguing that any extra cash would be better spend on improving services for patients than removing charges. He ordered a 5% cut in NHS staffing levels in the year 1953 and announced that the Guillebaud Inquiry had been set up to review costs in the NHS. [37]He got on well with the BMA perhaps because the big pay rise GP's had received after the Danckwerts report. Although he was a supporter of Health Centres, he wanted to try them first and see what worked best. The President of the Royal College of Surgeons called him "a true friend to doctors". He did not enjoy a similar relationship with dentists until in 1955 he announced a review of their pay.

In 1953 he announced a review of the cost of prescription drugs and a year later he launched a new drive to eliminate tuberculosis. Behind the scenes the

---

[35] Austerity Britain. D. Kynaston. Bloomsbury 20017
[36] Iain Macleod. Nigel Fisher. Andre Deutch.1973
[37] Guillebaud reported in January 1956 just as Macleod had left the Department of Health.

arguments about smoking and its dangers had been growing as the evidence began to accumulate. Alongside this concern was the spiralling costs of the NHS which made any loss of income from tobacco taxation problematic. In 1954 Macleod decided that a statement of some kind had to be made. During a press conference, throughout which he smoked incessantly, he acknowledged a possible link between smoking and lung cancer but added that more research was necessary before action could be justified. It would take another ten years and five more ministers before action was taken. [38] In February 1955 he asked a committee chaired by Henry Willink, a former Minister of Health, to work out the long-term requirement for doctors in the UK. Its membership included the great and the good of the time. It was to report in 1957.

In June 1955 he announced a ban on the manufacture and use of heroin which caused a major row with the BMA and provoked a hostile leader in The Times. He lost the Bill on a technicality in the House of Lords.

He appointed a Royal Commission on mental illness and mental deficiency which reported in 1957 to Walker-Smith his successor and led to the Mental Health Act in 1959.

Macleod was reappointed Minister of Health in 1955 when Eden became prime minister but was promoted to the Ministry of Labour and a seat in the Cabinet in December of the same year. In 1959 he became Secretary of State for the Colonies and is remembered for a speech at the Conservative Party Conference where he declared his belief in the "brotherhood of man". He was proud to be a One Nation Conservative and a great believer in the principles of the Beveridge Report.

He resigned from government in 1963 on a point of principle following the appointment of Lord Hume as prime minister. After a period in opposition and a spell as editor of The Spectator he returned to the opposition front bench in 1964 and in 1966 became shadow Chancellor of the Exchequer. In 1970 the Conservatives won a general election and Edward Heath appointed him as Chancellor. He died after only a month in office at the age of 56.

---

[38] The Nations Doctor. Sheard and Donaldson. Nuffield Trust 2005

He made no fundamental policy changes whilst Minister of Health, but he did act as a consolidator and a peacemaker with the medical profession. He got the best funding settlements he could with the Treasury and heightened awareness of the needs of the mentally ill. He was not afraid of controversial public health issues. Although he sometimes had strained relationships with political colleagues, he had excellent relationships with his civil servants and senior people in the NHS.

He was a hardworking and competent Minister of Health who understood the need to let the NHS develop naturally even in difficult economic circumstances.

[1913-1970]

ROBIN TURTON

December 1955-January 1957

Conservative

Robin Turton was born in North Yorkshire and educated at Eton and Oxford. He was called to the Bar in 1926 and awarded the Military Cross in 1942. At the 1929 general election he was elected MP for Thirsk and Malton a seat he held for the next 45 years. A long serving member of Parliament [Father of the House] he held a series of junior ministerial appointments between 1951 and 1955 and in December 1955 Anthony Eden appointed him as Minister of Health. He only served for 14 months. It was not at that time a post of cabinet rank.

He was described by some as the epitome of a Tory Squire and as a politician with a highly developed social conscience." Principle first, country second then party and constituents ". Some thought him to be a shy and diffident man.

He accepted the Guillebaud Report on the cost of the NHS which had recommended that no fundamental changes were required at that time to the structure of the NHS. The report showed that as a proportion of national wealth spending had reduced. What the NHS needed, he claimed, was the prospect of a period of stability.

He promoted polio vaccination at the prompting of John Charles the CMO. In May 1956 he departed from the official line by declaring "There is a causal link between smoking and lung cancer. That we know." He had a hard time with Hawton his Permanent Secretary who had been blocking anti-smoking policies at the behest of the Treasury. Hawton explained his minister's gaff as an oral slip. Another statement was prepared which had been approved in advance by Downing Street. More evidence was required before action could be justified.

He gave instructions that hospital farms with 40,000 acres and some pedigree herds be sold off claiming he had no powers to run them even if they were of therapeutic value. He blocked the transfer of the Epileptic Colonies into the NHS. He asked Sir Harry Platt the President of the Royal College of Surgeons to review the welfare of children in hospital. Platt reported in 1959.

He oversaw a large expansion in mental health and mental deficiency beds and coped with a ban on overtime by nurses working in these fields. He agreed to block plans to provide rimless spectacles for NHS patients.

He often tangled to his cost with Dr Edith Summerskill the opposition spokesperson on health. He strongly rebutted criticism of the Merit awards for Consultants against charges of nepotism. Like the rest of the Eden government he got involved in the politics of war as Britain invaded Egypt to secure the Suez Canal in October 1956.

He was strongly opposed to British membership of the European Community and on leaving ministerial office played a large part in the campaign to withdraw the UK from the Common Market. He had played a significant role in creating the system of legal aid for the poor. He was unflinching in whatever he saw as his duty.

He was a poor Minister of Health although his heart might have been in the right place.

He became Lord Tranmire in 1974 when he retired from the House of Commons.

[1903-1994]

DENNIS VOSPER

1957 [February-September]

Conservative

Dennis Vosper was born on the Wirral and after his studies at Cambridge worked in the family firm of Ships Store and Export Merchants in Liverpool. He was commissioned into the Cheshire regiment in 1939 reaching the rank of Major. He won the Runcorn seat in the 1950 general election and held it until 1964. He held office as Minister of Health in the Macmillan government for only eight months when he resigned on the grounds of ill health.

In April and May 1957 General Practitioners threatened to leave the NHS and provide services directly to patients for a standard fee unless the government increased their pay. An interim award resulted followed by the appointment of a Royal Commission chaired by Sir Harry Pilkington [39] which reported some three years later to Enoch Powell. The Royal Commission on Mental Health

---

[39] Royal Commission on the pay of Doctors and Dentists .1957-1960.Cmd 939.

reported but it was left to Walker-Smith his successor to respond. He resisted an attempt to refer the funding of the NHS to the Central Health Services Council claiming the Guillebaud Report had only recently been completed. Increases in GP prescribing, and the radioactive hazards of nuclear tests dominated his short ministerial career. Smoking inevitably raised its head again but Vosper and team stuck to the party line that this was a matter for individuals rather than the government.[40] He resigned in 1957 owing to illness. He was not in office long enough to make any material impact.

He resumed his ministerial career at the Home Office in 1959. He retired from the Commons in 1964 and moved to the House of Lords as Baron Runcorn.

[1916-1968]

DEREK WALKER–SMITH

September 1957-July 1960

Conservative

After achieving a first in History at Oxford Walker-Smith was called to the bar in 1934. Throughout his student days he had been a prolific producer of fiction, biographies and political tracts. During the war he was commissioned into the Royal Artillery and ended up on General Eisenhower's staff with the rank of Lieutenant Colonel. He won the Hertford seat in the 1945 general election[41] and made his early career as a parliamentarian becoming chair of the 1922 Committee in 1951. He also practiced at the Bar and was appointed Queen's Counsel in 1955.

He came to the Ministry of Health in 1957 after a short spell as Economic Secretary to the Treasury just as the NHS was entering its tenth year. He was the seventh Minister of Health in ten years. The economy was starting to grow again, and Harold MacMillan the Prime Minister told electors that "most of our people have never had it so good". However, behind the scenes Ministers were increasingly worried about inflation, regarded by Thorneycroft, the Chancellor as a serious threat to prosperity. Walker-Smith argued for a five-year hospital

---

[40] The statement was actually made by his PPS J K Vaughan-Smith as Vosper was in hospital at the time.
[41] His father who had been Director of Housing at the Ministry of Health lost his seat at Barrow in Furness at the same election.

building programme to match that for school building and in 1960 secured a ten-year plan with substantially increased capital investment. He welcomed the Royal Commission Report on Mental Health with its commitment away from institutional care towards care in the community and secured the passage of the Mental Health Act 1959 through Parliament. He accepted the Willink report on manpower planning for medicine which had concluded that with the influx of ex-servicemen there was a risk of oversupply. In what is now widely regarded as a mistake, although strongly supported at the time by the BMA, reductions were agreed for intakes to medical schools. Sir Harry Platt was asked to advice on the principles by which hospital medical staffing should be organised. It reported to Enoch Powell in 1961. He also accepted a report by Noel Hall on the grading of administrative staff in the NHS.

Polio vaccination was underway when he took up his post, but progress had been slow and limited to children from 2-5 years and expectant mothers. Other countries offered it to all citizens under 40. There were very heated debates in the House of Commons[42] in the first half of 1958 led by Edith Summerskill about the poor supply of the vaccines. An alternative Salk Vaccination had to be imported from Canada and the USA on a temporary basis until UK supply improved. There was also a related argument about a Russian vaccine for Multiple Sclerosis which Walker-Smith was not convinced about.

Health and Atomic Energy were recurrent lines of questioning as were cancer and tobacco. In this area he stuck very closely to the scientific advice he was given by the Medical Research Council that there was a higher mortality amongst people who continued to smoke than amongst those who gave smoking up. He also confirmed that tobacco had no radioactive content. [It was not until 1965 that cigarette advertising on TV was banned.] He pushed for international reciprocal agreements for emergency care. He initiated a joint review with the Joint Consultants Committee about the organisation of medical work in hospitals. It was during this time that the sanatoria for patients with TB began to shrink then close and then transfer to other specialties. On the tenth anniversary of the NHS he offered a positive view of progress but tempered the optimism with the comment that the NHS had

---

[42] Hansard 1/5/58. Vol 587 cc653-710

become an instrument for stimulating demand. An ageing population would, he explained, produce new patterns of disease which included coronary disease and cancer.

He received the Cranbrook report on maternity services in February 1958 and sent it out for comment which took almost two years. It had recommended that the NHS should plan for 70% of women to have their baby delivered in a hospital. He finally sent the report out as guidance for Health Authorities. It was to prove an important target for those working up the hospital plan that would be published later by Enoch Powell. He accepted the recommendations of the Platt report on the welfare of children in hospital which led to increased parental visiting rights.

His exchanges in the Commons could be sharp. In a response to Aneurin Bevin he said "I shall not weary the House again with a repetition of all the arguments which I have already put forward. Instead I intend to try to put before the House some new dishes and not merely a rechauffe of the spring menu which we had in the absence of the right honourable gentleman at that time."

He argued that "the people of this country were getting good value for the money being spent on the NHS".

In July 1960 he decided to leave the government and return to the law and his text book on building contracts. Macmillan accepted his resignation without regret and appointed Enoch Powell in his place. He stayed in the Commons until 1983 when he became Baron Broxbourne.

His three years in office as Minister of health turned out to be reasonably productive. His successor Enoch Powell got most of the credit for the groundwork he had undertaken on a capital programme for the NHS. His obituary[43] captures the essence of the man. He was a man who reached his full potential very early.

[1910-1992]

---

[43] Oxford Dictionary of National Biography.

ENOCH POWELL

July 1960-October 1963

Conservative

Enoch Powell was born in Stechford, Birmingham the son of a primary school teacher. He studied classics at Cambridge and then stayed on for a few years as a Fellow teaching philosophy. In 1937 he moved to Australia and became Professor of Greek at the University of Sidney. At the outbreak of war Powell immediately returned to the UK and joined the Royal Warwickshire Regiment. He was commissioned as an officer in 1940 and was almost immediately transferred to the Intelligence Corps. He served in the Middle East and helped plan the second battle of El Alamein. He then moved to join Mountbatten's staff in India. He ended the war as a Brigadier, the youngest in the British Army.

He entered Parliament in 1950 as MP for Wolverhampton South and quickly developed his reputation as one of the finest debaters of his generation. He had ministerial experience in Housing and as Financial Secretary to the Treasury prior to his appointment at Health in 1960. He was a monetarist. The idea that an NHS that diminished disease by prevention and cure would reduce long term demand was he thought a miscalculation of "sublime dimensions". Doctors, thinking how glorious it was that in the NHS patients did not have to pay them, because somebody else did, had fallen into a trap, he explained. That "somebody else" also had a limited purse. He believed in economy in public spending and that included the NHS. One of his early acts was to increase NHS charges.

He was not initially a member of the Cabinet [until July 1962].

He took over the ten-year capital programme for the NHS with gusto and a desire to have fewer beds in better hospitals. He persuaded the Treasury to reinvest some of the income from increased charges into the NHS capital programme. In January 1962 he published the Hospital Plan which contained within it 90 new hospitals and the upgrading of a further 134.[44] It was planned

---

[44] The Plan was revised and updated in 1963/1964/1966.

to cost £500m over ten years. The day of the District General Hospital had arrived. About 250 of these comprehensive hospitals providing all basic specialties under one roof were planned. They would each have between 600-800 beds.[45] The downside was that as they developed many small hospitals would have to close.

He shook the foundations of the mental health world with a speech in 1961. "There they stand, isolated, majestic, imperious, brooded over by giant water towers and chimney combined, rising unmistakable and daunting out of the countryside." The asylums must go, he said, and be replaced by community care which needed to be adequately funded.

Powell had an attempt at sorting out the specialist hospitals in London but ran into predictable opposition. He set up an Inquiry into the structure of nursing chaired by Brian Salmon a director of Lyons but had to leave it to his successor to implement when it reported in 1966.[46]

A Report by Sir Arthur Porritt, President of the Royal College of Surgeons came out in 1962 with strong support for the NHS. He recommended a single Area Board which was a precursor for the reorganisation that was to come some 12 years later.

Powell refused to set up a public Inquiry into Thalidomide and was thought to be unsympathetic to its victims. He did authorise free birth control services within the NHS

Like many ministers of health at this time he was drawn into the controversy about smoking. He had accepted the Royal College of Physicians report in 1962 that demonstrated "authoritatively and crushingly" the link between smoking and lung cancer. George Godber, his CMO, called the report wholly damning against cigarette smoking. The only argument now was how the habit could be broken.[47] Powell took the view that there was little he could do except "humbug" unless the Chancellor was willing to use fiscal weapons. It would, he said, be a new policy departure for a government to act to check habits, which

---

[45] The Bonham Carter Report in 1969 would recommend that the number of hospital beds in a DGH be increased to over 1000.
[46] It did not actually start work until 1963.
[47] On the State of the Public Health 1962.

when indulged in in excess would endanger health. It was a fallacy he argued with driving logic that tobacco was a source of revenue. The only source of revenue is the income of the citizen. One's duty as a minister, he explained, was to influence not dictate. If the State took responsibility it would erode the responsibility of the individual.[48] Decisions of this sort had to be left to the ordinary citizen. He faced a public health challenge in 1962 when smog returned to London claiming 750 lives.

He encouraged the recruitment of people from the West Indies to staff the NHS.[49]

He sought to balance the benefits of a national framework with local control. His Hospital Plan was an attempt "on a grand scale" to exploit the benefits of centralisation. The idea of non-ministerial management of an NHS wholly funded from general taxation was he said a chimera. The only way to separate medicine and politics would be to find an alternative funding source. He thought it possible to "square the circle "between central control and local management if there was mutual confidence between ministers and the Regional Hospital Boards and between the Regions and the field authorities. Bruce Frazer his Permanent Secretary was also of this view.

He had no great confrontations with the health professions and got on well with George Godber the CMO. He accepted the recommendations of the Royal Commission on doctors pay[50] chaired by Sir Harry Pilkington which led to the appointment of a Doctor's Pay Review Body. The doctors were by this time comfortable with the NHS as it consolidated their view of a medical system that treated the whole patient rather than a disease.[51] In 1961 he received a report from the Platt Committee which had been set up by Walker-Smith to review hospital staffing. He accepted the recommendation to appoint more Consultants and place a restriction on the number of junior medical staff. [52]

---

[48] Enoch Powell papers. Welcome library.SA/ASH/R.31.
[49] This programme had been initiated by his predecessor. Daily Telegraph 9/2/1998.
[50] Cmnd 939 1960
[51] Sir Arthur Porritt. President of the Royal College of Physicians 1962.
[52] He recommended an extra 400 per annum but this was rarely achieved.

He did not think that a doctor would ever make a good Minister of Health. If a doctor he or she would never be able to bring an outside view to health policy, he explained.

He survived MacMillan's night of the long knives in 1962 when a third of the cabinet were sacked.

He declined to continue in office after the October 1963 Election on a point of principle about how the succession from Macmillan to Douglas-Home had been handled. This was a matter of considerable regret to his many supporters in the NHS who had valued his clarity of thought, his directness and his energy. The medical profession was sad to see him leave.[53]

On leaving office he majored on the merits of free trade and market forces.

His Rivers of Blood speech in April 1968, for which he was sacked by Edward Heath from the Shadow Cabinet, killed off any prospect he may have had for further ministerial office despite huge public support. In a Parliamentary career of 37 years Powell had just fifteen months in Cabinet.

In 1974 he joined the Ulster Unionist party and won a seat in South Down, Northern Ireland. He lost this seat at the Bye Election in 1987.

In retirement he completed his version of the Greek New Testament. He died in 1998. The Guardian summed him up as follows; "Scholar, soldier, statesman, arch rebel, philosopher, poet".

[1912-1998]

ANTHONY BARBER

October 1963-October 1964

Conservative

Anthony Barber was born in Hull. He served with distinction in the Second World War but was captured in 1942 and sent to Stalag Luft 111 where he got

---

[53] British Medical Journal.26/10/1963 [11] 1012.

involved in several escapes including the one that was made into the film" The Wooden Horse". He studied law by correspondence course as a prisoner. After the war he practised at the Bar specialising in taxation.

In the 1951 general election he won the seat in Doncaster which had previously been a Labour stronghold. He held a series of junior ministerial posts which included a spell as parliamentary private secretary to Prime Minister Harold Macmillan. He entered the Douglas–Home Cabinet as Minister of Health in 1963 after Enoch Powell resigned. He only served a year in office.

The biggest problem he encountered as a Minister was the funding of general practice. The BMA had presented him with a huge claim for a 30% increase in remuneration in addition to the 14% recommended by the Doctors Review Body.

He appointed a working party chaired by Sir Bruce Frazer, his Permanent Secretary, which included both the BMA and the College of General Practitioners in its membership to review the problem. They largely completed their work by August 1984 and reported little enthusiasm for either a salaried service or fee for service payments to replace capitation. An outline agreement provided funding for practice premises and the employment of practice staff.

Barber rightly judged that the problems in general practice ran deeper than pay. He chided those patients who wasted doctor's time and attacked the bureaucracy that had built up around general practice. He was attracted to the idea of salaried general practice but was not prepared to impose it on the profession. Although the cost of general practice for the profession was reimbursed, he worried that the process of distribution was not spread in a manner that recognised the variation in actual costs between practices. He identified single handed practice as part of the problem.

Before any action could be finally agreed the 1964 general election intervened, and the problems passed to Kenneth Robinson his Labour successor.

Barber had encouraged local authorities to attach health visitors, midwives and district nurses to general practice which had begun the process of reshaping general practice and introducing multidisciplinary teams.

He announced an increase in the entry to medical schools and signed off a new medical school and teaching hospital for Nottingham.

He lost his seat in the 1964 general election but quickly returned to the House of Commons in 1965 after winning a bye election in Altrincham and Sale. When Edward Heath won the general election in 1970, he asked Barber to lead the team negotiating British entry into the common market but when Iain Macleod died suddenly Heath appointed him Chancellor of the Exchequer. He found himself caught between a Prime Minister set on a course of political expansion and a more cautious Treasury. He set about liberalising the banking system, introduced VAT and relaxed exchange controls. His policies led to what is now called the "Barber Boom" which led to inflationary pressures and the industrial unrest of the 1970's.

Barber was not a great political thinker but had a reputation as a hard-working problem solver with the gift of both clarity of thought and geniality. In private he was modest witty and charming. He was an inveterate smoker. He was heavily focused on general practice during his term of office. He was not long enough at Health to make an impact with ideas of his own.

He did not seek re-election in October 1974 and moved to the Lords as Baron Barber of Wentbridge.

[1920-2005.]

KENNETH ROBINSON

October 1964-November 1968

Labour

Son of a Doctor, Kenneth Robinson was born in Warrington but had to leave his school [Oundle] at the age of 15 on the death of his father. He worked in the insurance industry until he joined the Royal Navy in 1939 and spent much of the war on Atlantic convoys. Had his economic circumstances been different he would have entered medical school.

After the war he returned to the insurance industry and became a borough councillor at St Pancras. He won the St Pancras North seat in a bye election in 1949.

As a young MP he was regarded as modest, quiet and reliable and was made a whip until in 1954 he joined Aneurin Bevan in a revolt against the manufacture of the H bomb without Parliament's consent. He returned to the back benches. He was a member of the North West Metropolitan Regional Hospital Board from 1950 and chaired its mental health sub-committee. He was also Chair of the National Association for Mental Health [now MIND]. In this capacity he fought a long battle with the Church of Scientology which he regarded as a cult and socially harmful. He won a major libel action against them. He introduced the first major Commons debate on the Wolfenden Report which recommended ending criminalised consenting sex between men in private. He also put forward a bill to legalise abortion.[54]

In 1961 Hugh Gaitskell appointed him to be number two to Dr Edith Summerskill the opposition spokesman on health issues.

He was appointed Minister of Health by Harold Wilson after the general election in 1964. It was not a cabinet post. He got Shirley Williams as his junior minister. The government had a small majority of four.

He removed the patient contribution to the cost of prescriptions only to be forced to reinstate them in 1968 as an alternative to cuts in the hospital building programme. In practice the wide range of prescription charge exemptions reduced the Treasury yield to half of what they had anticipated.

As he came into office the link between cancer and heavy smoking [55] had been firmly established. Prior to 1962 there had been a lot of expert scepticism amongst scientists and doctors. In his report for 1964 George Godber the CMO had made it clear that in his view the rise in lung cancer deaths [56% more than ten years previously] was because of cigarette smoking. [56] Robinsons' concern was to stop young people smoking. He tried for a voluntary agreement with the tobacco industry but when the negotiations got nowhere, he

---

[54] It failed but the Abortion Act came into force in 1967 when he was Minister of Health.
[55] His emphasis was always on heavy smoking.
[56] On the State of the Public Health 1964.

persuaded the cabinet to proceed with legislation. Tobacco advertising was to be banned on television. It was not an easy decision as nobody wanted the government to seem illiberal or court political unpopularity. It was the first major step any government had taken since the dangers of smoking had been confirmed some eight years earlier.

General Practice was in serious decline when he assumed office and attempts were being made to draw them out of the NHS. GPs were regarded with something approaching contempt by hospital consultants. They were, one doctor alleged, the worst products of the medical school system. One fifth were still single handed. A working party chaired by Sir Bruce Frazer the Permanent Secretary had reported before the general election to Anthony Barber that radical change was needed. In 1965 Robinson published the GP Charter after eighteen months of negotiation with the BMA. He had led many of the negotiating meetings personally with George Godber the CMO and Arnold France the Permanent Secretary at his side. The Charter covered everything except pay which was a matter for the Doctors Review Body. Robinson would have preferred a salaried option but backed off in the search for a solution as had Bevan and Barber before him. When the deal was finally settled list sizes were to come down and capitation fees for the elderly were increased.[57] Finance was to be made available for practice premise development and there would be incentives for group practice and working in unattractive areas. Grants would support the employment of practice nurses and receptionists. When the deal was priced by the Review Body it produced a rise of thirty per cent in net remuneration. This caused a problem, but Robinson talked his colleagues' round. As James Callaghan the Chancellor at the time said" Kenneth had a profound understanding of the job he was doing, and we respected him because he knew what he was doing".

The Charter turned the tide in general practice[58] which was to experience a major renaissance. One consequence was that general practice was now firmly tied to the NHS. The picture with hospital consultants was brighter as their numbers spread across the country. The first heart transplant was evidenced as the continued growth in expertise in the acute sector of medicine.

---

[57] £10 million which was increased to £18million in 1971.
[58] G. Rivett. From Cradle to Grave. Kings Fund 1998

As the birth rate continued to increase the maternity services had come under pressure, particularly in London where the Emergency Bed Service found itself handling large numbers of obstetric cases.[59] More maternity beds were planned, and Maternity Liaison Committees created to improve coordination between all the organisations involved. The Abortion Act became law in 1967 and included a right for health professionals to claim a conscientious objection to participating.

Water supplies to Birmingham were fluoridised for the first time in 1964.

Barbara Robb's book *Sans Everything: A case to answer* created alarm and concern about the state of mental health services when it was published in 1967[60].Here Robinson made a serious error of judgement by "pooh poohing" the allegations and claiming that poor care was non-existent. It was left to Richard Crossman to act.

Robinson accepted Brian Salmon's review of nursing with its grades from 5 [staff nurse] to 10 [Chief Nursing Officer] but largely ignored the Platt report which had been commissioned by the RCN and had recommended that the academic entry level for registered nurse training should be increased and after two years in school there should be a year of supervised clinical practice. The enrolled nurse they recommended would follow a less elaborate apprenticeship type training. Under the Salmon plan nurses gave up their responsibilities for non-nursing duties including the management of nurse's homes and in some places cleaning services in order to concentrate on nursing duties.

The General Nursing Council reduced the number of nursing schools to those supported by the larger hospitals during this period of change.

He approved George Godber's "Cogwheel Report" on the organisation of medical work in hospitals. The first University Hospital Management Committees were created and sat alongside independent Boards of Governors. He got to grips with the Todd Report on medical education and the development of Post Graduate Medical Education.[61]. He negotiated an NHS

---

[59] 70% of babies were born in hospital in 1966.
[60] Barbara Robb was a trained psychotherapist.
[61] HM [64]69

pay bed reduction with the BMA not on ideological grounds but because they were under used. Local Authorities were permitted to provide free family planning services.

In November 1967 the Wilson government devalued the pound by 14% in order they said to get out of the straitjacket of boom and bust economics.

In 1968 Robinson published his plan to reorganise the NHS [The first Green Paper]. The tripartite structure of the NHS would he proposed be replaced by 40-50 Area Boards reporting directly to ministers. Central government must necessarily have an important guiding role but should not attempt itself to undertake the tasks of management in the field. The plans never materialised but led to a second green paper in 1970 from Richard Crossman.

In 1968 Harold Wilson decided to make Richard Crossman the supremo over all social services and Kenneth Robinson lost his job. He moved to Land and Planning a very disappointed man. Crossman thought that he had been Minister of Health for long enough.

He was a popular and much respected minister whose calmness and patience were to be an asset in building his relationships with his cabinet colleagues and the health professions. Sir Roy Calne remembered him as one of the few ministers of health that the medical profession has liked. The BMA thought him to be the most caring health minister they had ever had. John Horder now known as the father of modern general practice said, "he brought to the crisis a mind well prepared and a calmness and consideration". Godber talked about Robinson's quiet understanding and appreciation of medical problems; although he did not always give the doctors what they wanted. His philosophy was summed up in his frequent reference to a remark made by a St Pancras fireman talking about the London Blitz." We found out that we were all neighbours".

He left the government in 1969 to join British Steel as managing director of its personnel and social policy division. He later became chairman of the London Transport Executive and the Arts Council.

He was one of the very good ministers of health. He understood and was respected by health professionals and as a result took them with him as he reformed the NHS. His instincts about health policy were sound. He worked extremely well with his civil service colleagues with whom he formed one of the strongest teams the NHS has known. Some of his colleagues thought he got too close to the health professions. If he did, he always stuck to his socialist principles. His one misjudgement was his defensive reaction to criticisms about mental health services

1911-1996

RICHARD CROSSMAN

November 1968-June 1970

Labour

Richard Crossman, the son of a judge, studied classics at Oxford and went on to teach philosophy. He became a Fellow of New College Oxford at the age of 24. He was a councillor on Oxford City Council and leader of the Labour group from 1936-1940. His time during the war was spent in the Political Warfare Executive where he produced anti-Nazi propaganda. He later became assistant chief of the psychological warfare division of SHAEF[62]. His senior officer Sir Robert Bruce-Lockhart in a character assessment in 1945 seems to have caught the essence of the young Crossman. "He lacked team spirit and defied regulation, but his energy and agility of mind made a notable contribution to political warfare".

He entered the House of Commons in 1945 as MP for Coventry East, a seat he held until shortly before his death in 1974. He was very much to the political left of his party. He joined the National Executive in 1952 and became Chairman of the Labour Party in 1960-1961. He did not become a minister until 1964 when Harold Wilson appointed him Minister of Housing and Local Government where he had a turbulent but productive relationship with Dame

---

[62] Supreme Headquarters Allied Expeditionary Force.

Edith Sharp the formidable and long serving Permanent Secretary[63]. He took on the role of Secretary of State for Social Services in 1968 [a merger between Health and Social Security] where much of his energy went into a reform of pensions, a subject in which he claimed substantial expertise. He was based out of Whitehall in a shoddily built skyscraper next to the Tube Station at the Elephant and Castle.[64] He was an active member of Cabinet and took a considerable interest in trade union legislation. He increased NHS charges in 1969 but as a contribution to the cost of funding the comprehensive schools programme. He was interested in government rather than just health. In the early months of his term of office he seriously contemplated a review of the Consultant's Merit Award System which he regarded as pernicious and corrupt. However, George Godber the CMO predicted an unholy row with both the BMA and the Royal Medical Colleges so he backed off.[65] He did accept the Todd Report on Medical Education which amongst other changes recommended that the Royal Medical Colleges should authorise all medical training posts. Mandatory vocational training for general practice was to follow. He also accepted the Seebohm report which transformed welfare services into social services.

Mental health concerned him greatly on taking office mainly because of a series of critical reports [Ely, Farleigh[66], Sans Everything and others]. He had been appalled at a visit to Friern Barnet mental hospital. The staff were excellent but the conditions in which they had to work was appalling. In his car on the way back to the ministry he told Tam Dalyell; "I am responsible for running the worst kind of Dickensian, Victorian looney bin". He was determined to act and accelerate change. In 1969 he set up the Hospital Advisory Service to visit and inspect long stay hospitals. Its Director was accountable directly to the Secretary of State. The Ely Report[67] had been conducted by Geoffrey Howe[68]. Against the advice of officials Crossman agreed that it be published in full. The meeting inside the Department to sort out the Department's response was tense as Crossman was told by Baroness Serota his

---

[63] The Crossman Diaries.1979 Methuen.
[64] The DHHS had 6815 Headquarters staff in December 1969.
[65] Dick Crossman. A portrait. Tam Dalyell 1989.
[66] Farleigh in Somerset. A number of nurses were charged with ill treating patients. Cmnd 4557.
[67] Ely in Cardiff
[68] Later to become a senior cabinet minister but at this time a young barrister.

Minster of State that officials had known about the problems at Ely for some years but had done nothing about it. Ely, he suspected was not an isolated case. Everybody including those at the Region and in the Department of Health must share the blame he told his officials[69].From this point change in mental health begins to speed up.

A report by Bonham Carter had confirmed that the development of District General Hospitals which had been central to Enoch Powell's Hospital plan was still the right development path. Ideally patients should be treated at one hospital which had a comprehensive range of clinical expertise. There should be no more single specialty hospitals. The number of Consultants needed to be expanded to ensure none were single handed. From this point many single specialty hospitals were absorbed into District General Hospitals. A few like Great Ormond Street Hospital for Children survived.

He did have two big health projects. A white paper on reforming the NHS and another on improving services for the mentally handicapped.

As far as the NHS was concerned, he accepted the broad thrust of expert opinion that the NHS needed a more integrated structure broadly on the lines recommended by Kenneth Robinson. The Royal Commission on Local Government had recommended that Local Government should take over the NHS. Crossman's second green paper in February 1970 did not accept this advice but instead aligned the boundaries of new unified Area Health Authorities with local government with a Board membership that included many local people. One third of the membership was in the gift of local government. It was, thought Crossman, a miserable middle way but the best he could achieve[70]. It never happened because of the general election.

Clinical management had still not evolved at this stage and the medical profession strongly defended its right to clinical freedom. There was little if any interference with a doctor's clinical judgement about individual patients and little if any peer review of specialist practice.[71]

---

[69] Dame Kathleen Raven, the CNO, who took most of the pressure later expressed her relief that a minister was expressing concern at last.
[70] From Cradle to Grave. G. Rivett.

His work on improved services for the mentally handicapped produced a white paper for his successor in 1971. He agreed to create an NHS scientific service on the advice of Sir Solly Zuckerman.

Like many of his predecessors he had trouble with doctor's pay. In April 1970 the Independent Review Body chaired by Lord Kindersley had recommended a pay rise of 30%. The government blocked publication whilst they considered the implications. They referred half of the award to the National Board for Prices and Incomes. Crossman explained that the government was not rejecting the award just asking for a second opinion. Lord Kindersley and his Board resigned. The BMA introduced sanctions and threatened to strike. The matter was still not resolved at the time of the general election and it passed to Keith Joseph who withdrew the reference to the Prices and Incomes Board and created a new Pay Review body.

On the social security side Crossman laboured on a national superannuation scheme but it fell at the last hurdle when the 1970 general election was called. His relationship with his civil service colleagues was sometimes scratchy although like many of his predecessors, he got on well with George Godber the CMO. In his diaries he reflected his suspicion that he was not always told the whole truth. He constantly interrupted briefings. His passion for conspiratorial politics was sometimes divisive. He got at serious odds with Sir Clifford Jarrett his permanent secretary when Jarrett sought his agreement to taking on the role of President of the Society of Pensions Advisors on his retirement. Crossman was uneasy and raised the matter with the Prime Minister. [72] As it happened Jarrett was still in post when Labour lost the election. Keith Joseph asked him to stay on, but he retired as planned and went on to chair the Tobacco Research Council. Crossman's relationship with health authorities was also difficult at times. He later accused the 14 Regional Hospital Boards of behaving like semi-autonomous satraps towards a weak Persian Emperor.

After the general election Crossman became editor of the New Statesman until his contract was abruptly and prematurely terminated in March 1972. No doubt interpersonal problems were involved.

---

[71] Gordon Forsyth. Health Service Prospects. Nuffield Trust 1973.
[72] Crossman had his eyes on Sir Denis Barnes as Jarrett's replacement but was blocked by Barbara Castle who refused to let him move.

Crossman died in April 1974. Barbara Castle said" Crossman has died, and a great abrasive and tonic force has gone." Tam Dalyell who was his PPS described his political career as precocious.

He was not one of the great Ministers of Health, but he made his reputation for radical thinking in the wider government. He did lift the level of policy thinking inside the Ministry and the NHS about mental health and mental handicap. Much of what he started in health was passed onto his predecessor after the general election in 1970.

[1907-1974]

KEITH JOSEPH

June 1970- March1974

Conservative

Keith Joseph was the son of Samuel Joseph who owned and built up Bovis the building company. His father had been created a Baronet in 1943 after completing his term of office as Lord Mayor of London. Keith Joseph inherited the baronetcy on the death of his father in 1944.

After school at Harrow, Joseph went to Oxford where he secured a first-class honours degree in Jurisprudence. In 1939 he joined the Royal Artillery. He rose to the rank of captain and was mentioned in dispatches. At the end of the War he was called to the Bar and became a Director of Bovis.[73] He entered Parliament in 1956 as MP for Leeds North East a seat he held until he retired

---

[73] He became Chairman of Bovis in 1958.

from Parliament in 1987.He had a first-class mind and was to set new standards for public frankness. He was an advocate of what he called civilised conservatism. Margaret Thatcher said it was Joseph who really "began to turn the intellectual tide against socialism".[74] He co-founded the Foundation for Management Education in 1960.

Joseph had entered the Harold Macmillan Cabinet as Minister of Housing and Local Government [75] in 1962 and introduced a massive programme of council house building.

He was appointed Secretary of State for Social Services in June 1970 in the government of Edward Heath. His appointment was a surprise as in opposition he had shadowed Industry and gained a reputation for extolling free market ideas. He was to join a government that was to have a turbulent three and a half years with a Prime Minister preoccupied with industrial strife, entry into the EEC and the troubles in Northern Ireland. It was a government determined to reduce taxes, cut the size of the public sector and stop rescuing industrial lame ducks. Joseph was to have a relatively free hand with the health portfolio.

Not everybody welcomed his appointment. Barbara Castle argued "that the NHS was in the hands of the arch apostle of an abrasive new brand of Toryism".

His term of office had only just begun when the Chancellor of the Exchequer reduced the standard rate of tax and announced a steep increase in prescription charges. He also withdrew free school milk for the over sevens which was to cause problems for Margaret Thatcher then at Education.

Joseph's term of office was dominated by the 1974 reorganisation of the NHS. In his consultative paper of 1971 he accepted many of the ideas in Crossman's green paper but elected to keep a regional tier[76].Local authorities retained some services, but their role was much diminished. The members of Health Authorities would be chosen for their management experience. McKinsey, the management consultants, advised on the detailed management structures which would be based on consensus management and multidisciplinary teams.[77]T

---

[74] Joseph. Morrison Hachrow. Macmillan 1989
[75] The post also included Minister for Welsh Affairs.
[76] 14 Regional Health Authorities, 90 Area Heath Authorities with 192 operational districts.

hey were very detailed, very complex and mandatory all over the country. These teams brought medicine and nursing firmly into the management orbit. The top teams included a Consultant, General Practitioner, Community Physician and a senior Nurse.

The Lancet welcomed the plan with its emphasis on integration and clinical engagement; the future they thought looked bright.

From 1972 working parties comprising all three tripartite authorities prepared for change. There was a major clear out of senior staff as everybody had to compete for a job in the new structures. It was a time of turmoil and excitement in the NHS managerial community. Beneath the regional tier were Area Health Authorities [often matching county boundaries e.g. Cheshire, Humberside or Derbyshire] with a varying number of multidisciplinary teams who were tasked with day to day management.[78] A Staff Commission was appointed to handle the transfer of staff to the new organisations. Community Health Councils were created. The post of Medical Officer of Health disappeared. The specialty of Community Medicine was created. The teaching hospitals which had enjoyed a direct line to the ministry since 1948 were swept under the wings of the Regional Hospital Boards and Boards of Governors disappeared. There was strong but mistaken belief that reorganising the management structure would increase efficiency in the NHS. The NHS Reorganisation Act gained Royal Assent on 5th April 1973 the twenty fifth anniversary of the creation of the NHS.

Vesting day was 1st April 1974 but by that date Barbara Castle was in Office following a Labour election victory in March. She left the reforms largely intact, but they did not survive for long. They were widely regarded as a failure.

Joseph published Better Service for the Mentally Handicapped in 1971 which was to signal a long term move away from institutional care and the build-up of community services[79]. In January 1971 local authorities created social service committees who appointed Directors of Social Service. He targeted the

---

[77] The Grey Book set out detailed management structures which had to be applied across the NHS.

[78] Cheshire Area Health Authority had five operational districts. Chester, Warrington, Halton, Macclesfield and Crewe.

[79] Better services for the mentally ill would be published by Barbara Castle in 1975.

additional funds secured for the NHS to improving services for the elderly and the mentally ill and encouraged local authorities to join him in a determined attempt to replace the former poor law institutions that were still being used as old people's homes.[80]

Mental health continued to be a problem as further inquiry reports demonstrated how bad some of the long stay institutions had become. In a move to strengthen their management some were merged with local acute services into new combined Hospital Management Committees. The pressure to close the large asylums altogether increased sharply.

The scientific evidence about the dangers of smoking had continued to accumulate and Joseph asked all hospitals to investigate the practicalities of a ban. Progress was slow.

He became embroiled in a very public row about contraception. He believed that it should be free on the NHS. The problem was money. The debate however focused on morality and social responsibility and Joseph's social principles began to emerge more clearly. He wanted to break what he called the cycle of deprivation in which unwanted children were one manifestation. He explained "when a child is deprived of constant love and guidance, he is deprived of a background most likely to lead to stability and maturity[81]." In the end he agreed that contraception would be available for the normal prescription charge.[82]

1971 saw the publication of the Asa Briggs report on nursing which recommended a unified statutory registration body for the profession, more undergraduate nursing degree courses, and colleges of nursing and continuing professional education. These ideas were full of practical and legal problems so nothing much happened during Joseph's term of office.[83]

He commissioned the Court Committee to review child health services. It reported in 1976 after he had left office.

---

[80] DHSS Annual Report 1971.
[81] Keith Joseph. A Single Mind. Halcrow. Macmillan 1989.
[82] The cost to the NHS was around £3m.
[83] The recommendations concerning training were approved in 1975 by Barbara Castle and led to the Nurses and Midwives Act 1975.

General practice was continuing to grow and evolve as group practice became more popular and local authorities attached their community nursing staff, midwives and health visitors to general practice in greater numbers.[84] The Harvard Davies report gave further impetus to the development of group practice.

Joseph accepted the Peel[85] report on maternity services which had recommended that all deliveries should take place in hospital. Domiciliary midwifery services reduced almost overnight. The evidence base for this report was later judged to be weak by experienced researchers.

Joseph encouraged scientific inquiry and research with the strong support of George Godber the CMO. One of the results was the Cochrane paper on Effectiveness and Efficiency in Medicine. Health authorities were encouraged to take computing beyond payroll and accounting and Regional Health Authorities began to build up quite large computing departments and experiment with clinical applications such as screening.

His White Paper on Pensions reform came out in September 1971. During his period of office he extended pension rights to young widows and created a new invalid allowance for the severely disabled.

Throughout the years of the Heath government industrial action in both the public and private sectors was a major problem with the economy in a ferment of industrial unrest. Unemployment reached 1 million for the first time since 1947.

1970 turned out to be the worst year for days lost since 1926. The government decided to change the law to inhibit unofficial strikes. The Industrial Relations Act became law in the summer of 1971 and the Industrial Relations Court started to operate in January 1972.

There was much discontent about pay in the NHS where union membership had been growing rapidly. In 1972, during the preparations for the 1974 reorganisation, ancillary staff [porters, cleaners, catering and laundry staff] started to take strike action, some of it unofficial. 750 hospitals became

---

[84] In October 1971 the number of principals in general practice in England was 19,374 after the greatest annual increase in ten years.
[85] Peel was a former President of the Royal College of Obstetricians and Gynaecologists

involved. The initial cause was a break in the long-standing link between their pay and the pay of ancillary workers in local government. Non-emergency surgery was effectively stopped and in some parts of the country emergency services were threatened. The emotional barrier against strike action in the NHS had been breached and was to lead to a decade of sporadic industrial action. Strike action by the miners who had started to deploy flying pickets coincided with the action in the NHS. The oil crisis in 1973 added to the government's problems and led eventually to Edward Heath enforcing a three-day week for the use of electricity on British industry. It was lifted on the 8th March 1974 immediately after his defeat in the General Election.

Negotiations about a new consultant's contract started in 1972 and militant consultant groups started to threaten industrial action. A breakaway organisation, the Regional Hospital Consultants Association, put pressure on BMA negotiators. The BMA demanded a closed contract which specified a consultant's time commitment to the NHS and overtime payments when these limits were exceeded. Junior doctors began to campaign for shorter hours. All these problems were unresolved when the general election was called and lay in the in tray for Barbara Castle and David Owen.

Joseph has been described as accessible, open minded, inquisitive, industrious and less abrasive than his predecessor Richard Crossman. He always believed that the power of reason would solve most problems. Others judged him to be a lion in opposition and a lamb in government. His intensely nervous disposition was related to a chronic, persistent and often painful set of physical ailments. [86]

He operated well with his civil servants who liked and respected him. He listened closely to the advice offered by Philip Rogers his Permanent Secretary and George Godber the CMO. He always took a note pad with him on ministerial visits.

After the election defeat in 1974 Joseph chose not to join the shadow cabinet and instead created the Centre for Policy Studies with Margaret Thatcher who had become a staunch ally.

---

[86] Oxford Dictionary of National Biography.

Joseph was an active Minster of Health whose energies were taken up with a major reorganisation that eventually failed. The concept of service integration had been right but the management structure that came with it was hopelessly complex and bureaucratic. He judged himself to have been a bad member of Heath's cabinet "in the sense that I was obsessed with my departmental job and never raised my head to recognise, let alone protest about, the monetary incontinence which we adopted."[87]

Joseph returned to government in 1979 as Secretary of State for Industry and then in 1981 Secretary of State for Education and Science.

In 1987 he became Baron Joseph of Portsoken in the City of London.

[1918-1994]

BARBARA CASTLE

March 1974-April 1976

Labour

Barbara Castle was born into a politically active family. Her father, a tax inspector, was editor of the Bradford Pioneer the city's socialist newspaper. Her mother was a Labour Councillor in Bradford. She joined the Labour Party as a teenager. She read PPE at Oxford where she was Treasurer of the Oxford University Labour Club. During the war she worked at the Ministry of Food and was an air raid warden during the Blitz.

In 1945 she was elected MP for Blackburn. At 34 she was the youngest woman in the Commons She became a high profile Bevanite and became quite close to

---

[87] The Independent.13.11.1987.

Nye Bevan and Jenny Lee his wife. From 1945-47 she served as Parliamentary Private Secretary to both Stafford Cripps and Harold Wilson when they were at the Board of Trade. In 1949 she served her year as Chairman of the Labour Party.

After a turbulent time as Minister for Transport where she introduced the breathalyser test she moved to the post of First Secretary of State under Harold Wilson and started the process of reforming the Trade Unions which met with stiff opposition from both Trade Unions and the Parliamentary Labour Party.[88] In the end the cabinet "ratted"[89] on her proposals and sued for peace with the TUC. She intervened personally in the Ford sewing machinists strike in 1968 which focused on equal pay. [90] In March 1974 she took office as Secretary of State for Social Services with Dr. David Owen as her deputy.

Keith Joseph's reorganisation of the NHS was about to start in a few weeks after years of preparation. Phillip Rogers the Permanent Secretary told Castle and Owen that the reorganisation could be stopped but it would throw the NHS into chaos. They decided to let it proceed. It was too late to unscramble Joseph's eggs she later explained.

The principle of integrating the three arms of the NHS was not controversial but the management structure that came with it was very complicated and bureaucratic. The new multidisciplinary management teams had to work on a consensus basis. Most worked well but a few collapsed because of poor interpersonal relationships within the teams. The unit managers who interfaced most directly with the Consultants felt disempowered because of the plethora of district wide functional managers above them [District Catering Managers, District Physiotherapists etc.]. The Consultants complained that it was difficult to get decisions made as the District and Area tiers argued about priorities. It all started to unravel quite quickly.

In May 1974 Castle added local authority members to the Boards of the Regional Health Authorities and increased the proportion of local authority seats on Area Health Authorities from a quarter to a third.[91]

---

[88] In Place of Strife. 1969.Cmnd 3888.
[89] According to Harold Wilson
[90] This led to her pushing through the Equal Pay Act in 1970.
[91] Democracy in the NHS

When Castle took office, the NHS was in an expanding phase and expenditure rose in 1974-75 to 5.4% of GNP.[92] Despite this the NHS had a constant mood of crisis about it. It was getting better but feeling worse. However, the economic tide was on the turn. Anthony Crosland put it to local government officers in May 1975 "The party is over". In September 1976, by which time David Ennals was in post, Denis Healy had to ask the International Monetary Fund for a loan.

Despite the gloomy financial outlook Castle secured some increases in social security benefits. The NHS however found its capital programme decimated. David Owen had to tour the country explaining to health authorities why their development schemes could not proceed. On a visit to Leeds he suggested that the plans for a new General Infirmary had a top floor removed to reduce cost. Many other schemes had to be broken down into small phases.

Community Hospitals were however given a lifesaving push when their role in serving patients that did not need the high technology of the DGH was outlined.

Industrial relations conflict in the NHS was a constant problem during Castle's term of office. In April 1975 she had commissioned Lord McCarthy to review the pay bargaining machinery in the NHS.[93]

She had declared quite early on that she planned to phase private practice out of NHS hospitals and despite warnings from her Permanent Secretary and CMO about the likely reaction from the BMA decided to proceed. It was a piece of unfinished Bevan business. She explained her position in a debate in the Commons "The issue before us is whether the facilities of the NHS which are supposed to be available on the principle of medical priority should contain facilities that were available on a different principle" i.e. the ability of the patient to pay.[94]

She personally brokered a deal at the new Charing Cross Hospital in June 1974 where the local NUPE branch was threatening to withdraw all services from the private wing. She promised the trade union that she would remove pay

---

[92] This would not continue as the last three months of 1973 saw the OPEC countries embargo the sale of oil with its consequential impact on Western economies.
[93] It reported to David Ennals in December 1976.
[94] The New Politics of the NHS. Rudolf Klein. Radcliffe Publishing.

beds from within the NHS even though the number of pay beds had been slowly declining.[95]

In January 1975 consultants began to work to contract.

A cabinet discussion in 1975 [96] explained:

"The Secretary of State was caught between two fires. On the one hand there were the doctors who were in a highly militant mood and on the other were the NHS Trade Unions amongst whose members feeling against pay beds was running very high". It was decided to introduce a short Bill which would establish beyond doubt the power of the Secretary of State to phase out pay beds from the NHS and fix a timetable for doing this. It was also proposed that the Bill included interim powers to require all private hospital development to be subject to the approval of the Secretary of State. Barbara Castle reported that the Consultants had already announced their intention to provide only emergency care unless the whole issue of private practice was referred to the promised Royal Commission on the NHS. The Cabinet discussion reflected the concern that the interim powers might give the impression that the government wanted to phase out private practice altogether when what the government wanted was a thriving private health sector but one that was separated from the NHS. Further negotiation was necessary the Cabinet concluded".[97]

These further discussions took place in the flat of Lord Goodman a distinguished solicitor and a deal was eventually struck whereby private beds would eventually be phased out of the NHS using an independent Board which would ensure that the changes would be compensated by new developments in the private hospital sector. Henry Yellowlees the CMO was excluded from these discussions which caused great offence and severely strained his relationship with Barbara Castle.

A Bill to regulate private practice was fought through Parliament and received Royal Assent in November 1976.

---

[95] 7188 in 1956 to 4500 in 1974. Less than 1% of NHS beds.
[96] Cabinet Minute, National Archives CAB 128/57/21.
[97] Any Consultant could do private practice up to 10% of NHS salary, but if over three years this limit was exceeded the Consultant was required to take a maximum part time contract losing one eleventh of his NHS salary with no diminution of NHS workload. In 1976 42.8% of NHS Consultants worked part-time.

She and David Owen failed to get a final settlement to the negotiations about Consultants pay and had to concede a pay rise averaging 30% in April 1975. She did however make real progress with nurses and other professional staff when she appointed Lord Halsbury to review their pay which produced an average pay rise of 30%. The Nursing Unions never forgot her role in this dispute and years later still remembered her as a hero. Behind the scenes work continued on the potentially extended role of the nurse which would come to fruition years later. There was a series of nasty local skirmishes about the implementation of the national junior doctors' overtime deal towards the end of 1975. Some Senior Registrars were earning more than their Consultant bosses.

She launched Better Services for the Mentally Ill in 1975, work that had started under her predecessor Keith Joseph, and followed this up with a review by Peggy Jay of mental handicap nursing. Like several other reports, they were to land eventually on the desk of her successor David Ennals.

In October 1975 Harold Wilson announced that there would be a Royal Commission on the NHS. This might have been a genuine attempt to find a way forward, but it was also a convenient way of moving some difficult issues into the long grass. Its brief under the chair of Sir Alec Merrison was "to consider in the interests of both the patients and those who work in the NHS the best use and management of the financial and manpower resources of the NHS. The brief covered the whole of the UK.[98]

Just before she left office the Department published, for the first time, a consultation document on the developmental priorities for both health and social services. Primary Care was set to rise by 3.8% a year as were services for both the elderly, mentally ill and for people with mental handicap. However acute services would have to be constrained to 1.2% which was a considerable reduction in growth compared to previous years. Between 1970 and 1974 the NHS had recruited an extra 5000 doctors most of them in the acute sector.

To complicate matters she announced in May 1975 that she had appointed a working party to review the allocation of both revenue and capital funds between NHS regions. There was clearly an imbalance between the London

---

[98] The Royal Commission reported in July 1979.

regions and most of the rest of the country.[99] Although this would not have been top of her personal agenda it turned out to be one of most important reforms she initiated. The diverted funds revitalised NHS services in the midlands and the north of England.[100]

Barbara Castle made several important changes to the social security rules including the introduction of the mobility allowance, the rule that pensions should rise in line with average earnings and the payment of child benefit to mothers.

When James Callaghan took over as Prime Minister in 1976 Barbara Castle lost her ministerial post and her place in Cabinet. In December 1975 just before leaving office she reviewed the NHS for the Fabian Society[101]. She reviewed the fight that Bevan had had in its creation. The clash over private beds was unfinished business from that era. The row represented a row between those who wanted to complete the work of Bevan in ensuring that no one should be debarred from getting the best treatment because they could not afford to pay and those who believed that any expansion of the NHS would have to be funded privately.

She left Westminster at the 1979 general election and very quickly became an MEP for Greater Manchester and Leader of the Labour Group in Strasbourg.

In 1990 she entered the Lords as Baroness Castle of Blackburn.

Barbara Castle was not an outstanding Secretary of State. She never managed to build an effective relationship with the medical profession despite having Dr David Owen as her deputy. She did not trust the medical staff in the Ministry who she thought were in the pay of the BMA. She resisted an extension to the term of office of her Permanent Secretary Phillip Rogers who retired in February 1975. Her action on private practice in the NHS was a major distraction from the real health agenda. She was very politically focused and would always fight battles to uphold her socialist principles. She was better at fighting causes than making policy.

Politics was her life not the NHS.

---

[99] RAWP report which was published in September 1976.
[100] For the most part equalisation was achieved by varying growth levels rather that direct cuts.
[101] NHS revisited. Fabian Tract 440. December 1975.

[1910- 2002.]

DAVID ENNALS

April 1976-May 1979

Labour

David Ennals was born in Walsall in the Black Country. On leaving school he took up an English-Speaking Union scholarship in the USA. On his return he worked briefly as a journalist until he was old enough to enrol in the Staffordshire Regiment. During the invasion of Normandy, he was wounded, captured and held prisoner in a German hospital. For a long time, he was missing presumed dead.[102]

He first stood, unsuccessfully, for Parliament in 1950 and 1951 as a Liberal candidate. He then became the Secretary of the United Nations Association in 1952 before moving in 1957 to the Labour Party headquarters as International Secretary a post with little if any support. In this role, be built up a close relationship with Harold Wilson.

In 1964 he secured a seat in Parliament as MP for Dover. After several junior posts at Defence and the Home Office Harold Wilson appointed him Minister of State under Richard Crossman. He worked well with Crossman who had a high opinion of his skills as a minister.[103] Both had a strong interest in mental health. He transferred to social security in 1969 and Bea Serota took his place at health.

He lost his seat at the 1970 general election and became campaign director for MIND. He returned to Parliament in 1974 as MP for Norwich North and became Minister of State at the Foreign Office. When James Callaghan took

---

[102] Oxford Dictionary of National Biography.
[103] The Crossman Diaries. Hamilton Cape 1979

over as Prime Minister in 1976 Ennals hoped he might become Foreign Secretary but instead he became Secretary of State for Social Services.

It was a difficult time as the Callaghan government sought to constrain public expenditure by imposing strict limits on pay and costs. Denis Healey had had to secure a loan from the IMF in December 1976.Inflation was rampant reaching a peak of 26.9% in the year up to August 1979.Strict cash limits were imposed on public sector organisations including the NHS.

One of his first tasks was to drastically cut the promised benefits under the Child Benefit Scheme. Barbara Castle was furious and attacked him in the Commons for "abandoning one of the Party's major reforms".[104]

On the health side one of his first tasks was to sign off the detailed arrangements for the work of the Royal Commission on the NHS. This significantly inhibited the flow of new policy and effectively blocked any further reorganisation. Its report was presented to Patrick Jenkin in July 1979 after Ennals had left office. Ennals did however accept a report from three regional chairman commissioned by David Owen into the relationship between the English NHS regions and the DHSS. The Region's role was to be strengthened at the expense of the Department of Health.

He stuck broadly to Castle's Priorities Policy which squeezed the acute hospital sector to allow growth in mental health and the other Cinderella services. His version "The Way Forward" was less specific about relative rates of increase but still encouraged debate about national priorities. He asked Sir Douglas Black the President of the Royal College of Physicians to look at health inequalities.[105] He did not pursue Barbara Castle's attack on private practice in the NHS with any fervour but did establish the Health Services Board to manage the phase out of private beds from the NHS.

He published a paper on medical manpower for public comment which had concluded that the NHS could afford an increase in medical staffing at the rate of 1-2% a year. Negotiations about a new Consultant contract initiated in early 1977 rumbled on into 1978.

---

[104] Hansard 5C.912.1975-6.287.
[105] The Black Report was published in 1980 and linked poverty and ill health. It was to prove very controversial.

In September 1976 the Resource Allocation Working Party Report [RAWP] report landed on his desk recommending a long-term shift in the allocation of both revenue and capital between NHS regions. London was badly affected as revenue began to move north and the NHS in the capital had to survive with little if any real growth.[106] In the northern regions plans for new District General Hospitals were accelerated. Improving primary health care was part of a wider government initiative focused on the inner cities and produced some increased funding

The McCarthy report on pay negotiation in the NHS also arrived on his desk in 1976 and he was able to make some sensible changes to the Whitley system for pay determination in the NHS. However, this did little to stem the industrial action which had almost become endemic within the NHS and the whole of the public sector as the Callaghan government capped pay rises. He was in post during the winter of discontent and in January in 1979 had to tell Parliament that half of English hospitals were only able to offer emergency care because of industrial action. The 22nd January 1979 saw the biggest strike in the UK since the general strike of 1926.[107]

The dangers of smoking, an ever-present issue for Ministers of Health at this time came to the fore when the second report of the Royal College of Physicians was published in 1977.The report attributed more than 25 thousand premature deaths of people between the ages of 35-64 to smoking. The ban on cigarette advertising had been in place since 1965 and had been extended to independent radio stations in 1973.In 1977 stronger warnings were put on packs of cigarettes. At last government was reacting to the clinical evidence of harm.

In his drive for efficiency in the NHS he commissioned a study into NHS supplies which led to a push for greater standardisation of goods within the system and a computer-based information and ordering systems. He changed the rules about land transactions in the NHS which allowed some or all the sale income to be reinvested locally rather than being returned to a national pot.

---

[106] Rawp took account of population size and make up as well as morbidity.
[107] This was the time when the grave diggers went on strike in Liverpool.

He also dealt with the Jay report into mental handicap nursing which called for more nurses and better training. The Court Report also recommended changes to Child Health when it was published in December 1976. The Normansfield Report about cruelty to patients, weak management and a difficult Medical Superintendent reported in November 1978 and appalled him.

He lost his seat once again in the 1979 general election.

Following his exit from Parliament he re-established his connection with MIND first as Chairman and later as President. He entered the Lords as Baron Ennals of Norwich in 1983 and became his party's spokesman on health.

He was a popular and hardworking minister who exerted his influence without the need for pitched battles. He had a high level of personal energy and a persistently overbooked diary. Patrick Nairne his permanent secretary described him as a very caring minister who was skilful in dealing with his senior colleagues. Tam Dalyell thought him to be more at ease with civil servants than the Parliamentary Labour Party. His time in office was dominated by a tough industrial relations scene[108] and any policy drive he may have wanted to mount was blunted by the work of the Royal Commission.

He was a popular and competent Secretary of State although his health sometimes let him down.

1922-1995

PATRICK JENKIN

May 1979- September 1981

Conservative

---

[108] He was himself ill at the height of the industrial action.

Patrick Jenkin read law at Cambridge although his education was interrupted by his national service with the Queens Own Cameron Highlanders. He was called to the Bar in 1952 and succeeded Winston Churchill as the MP for Woodford from 1964. He quickly began to speak for the Opposition on economic and trade affairs and became Chief Secretary to the Treasury in the Heath government between 1970 and 1974.

In 1979 Margaret Thatcher made him Secretary of State for Social Services a post he had been shadowing for three years. Whilst in opposition he had concluded that it would be possible to provide an NHS through a publicly provided and publicly administered health insurance scheme. On appointment he shared his ideas with Patrick Nairne the Permanent Secretary who was not enthusiastic and there were doubts that Mrs Thatcher would have supported the idea. It was dropped with no public debate.[109]

He began, according to Margaret Thatcher, the process of bringing the finances of health and social services within the constraints of what the ordinary people of England could afford to pay.[110] He had been enthusiastic about the contribution health insurance could make to the NHS. He found the NHS in the midst of a period of difficult industrial unrest which reflected problems in the wider economy[111]. Union membership in the NHS had been expanding since the early 1970s and with it had come a growth in shop stewards and union convenors.[112] Industrial action had become commonplace but grew in intensity during the winter of discontent in 1978/9. The first three months of 1979 the trade unions fought a bitter battle against low pay in the public sector. Their favoured tactics were overtime bans, no cleaning in non-clinical areas, no catering for management meetings or special functions, laundry for emergency care only. By and large the unions were careful not to put emergency services at risk although unofficial action sometimes came close.

Jenkin appointed Professor Roger Dyson an expert in industrial relations as his political advisor. Health Authorities were told how they were expected to respond to threats of industrial action. Management had to toughen up. He

---

[109] Rejuvenate or Retire. Views of the NHS at sixty. Nuffield Trust.
[110] Extract from Thatcher letter on Jenkins resignation from government. September 1985.
[111] Unemployment was over two million the highest since 1935.
[112] By 1977 the number of staff in the NHS was over one million.

put Commissioners into Lambeth, Southwark and Lewisham when the Area Health Authority refused to operate within their cash limit. He considered doing the same thing in Liverpool where Derek Hatton of Militant Tendency was in control[113]. It turned out that the Direction that authorised the Commissioners to act was illegal and Jenkin was forced to steer an NHS [Invalid Direction] Bill through Parliament during March 1980.

He gave the nurses a large pay award but not as much as the Clegg Commission had recommended. He allowed GPs to employ their wives as secretaries and assistants and settled the long running battle with the BMA about private practice in the NHS by shutting down the Board that regulated pay beds. With the support of Thatcher and Howe he protected the NHS from any heavy cuts although the NHS in the South East was beginning to suffer from the reallocation of resources between regions [RAWP].

The Royal Commission Report when it was published in July 1979 had few radical recommendations. "Steady as you go" was the Commission's broad advice. "The NHS was not suffering from a mortal disease susceptible only to heroic surgery". Primary Care was provided to a good standard but could be improved. A salaried option in general practice would add value. The DGH concept was correct but nucleus hospitals could speed up modernisation. The removal of private practice from the NHS was a distraction. Relationships between the NHS and Local Authorities varied from excellent to indifferent but transferring the NHS to Local Government would not be a good idea.

The government's response to the Royal Commission came out in December 1979 under the heading Patients First. Jenkin took the Commission's advice in deciding against whole scale reorganisation, but he was determined to simplify the NHS structure and he removed the area tier of management and created District Health Authorities which for the most part matched the boundaries of the former operational districts. He set a population limit of 500,000 for the new district authorities. He also dismantled much of the functional management that had developed in the system and returned basic services such as catering to local managers. Despite the opposition from the BMA doctor's contracts were to be moved from RHAs to local District Health

---

[113] In the end the City Council bowed to Jenkin's instructions.

Authorities. Management costs were expected to reduce by 10% in what turned out to be a particularly brutal reorganisation that took forever to complete[114]. Jenkin also returned to an old idea from the 1960's that Regional Health Authorities should be consortia of districts, but this never materialised. In these times a Secretary of State had few inhibitions about getting directly involved in the detail of NHS management and imposing his solutions all over the country. One Royal Commission recommendation that was not accepted was the one to make social care free. Social care would remain means tested.[115]

In May 1980 Gerard Vaughan his minister of state issued a consultation paper on the future pattern of hospital services. The basic thrust of the paper was to limit the size of District General Hospitals to around 600 beds and encourage the retention of small rural hospitals. The cottage hospital had been saved again for a while. Vaughan an experienced physician did not enjoy a reputation for decisiveness or political acumen, but he was a strong supporter of Mrs Thatcher.[116] He argued publicly for an extension of private health insurance, but his ideas gained no traction with his colleagues.

Jenkin delayed publication of the Black Report on the link between poverty and health which had been finished before the election until August Bank Holiday 1980.Although this delay has been blamed on a political dissatisfaction with its conclusions the truth was that officials had not completed their submissions to Jenkin until May 1980 and were not at all enthusiastic quoting massively increased public expenditure and poor research.[117] It made little short term impact on policy but triggered a worldwide debate.

He asked Edith Korner to review NHS information services and her report shaped the system for the next decade. Alongside this work performance indicators were being developed which exposed a wide variation in clinical practice across the NHS. Lengths of stay for routine procedures such as cataract removal were enormous. General surgery day case rates ranged from 2% to 42% in 1985.Meanwhile in Cambridgeshire Terence English was

---

[114] The DHHS had predicted 435 early retirements. When the dust had settled it was almost 3000.
[115] A similar recommendation was made by another Royal Commission in 2000.
[116] Ken Clarke.
[117] Socialist Medical Association.

restarting the heart transplant programme having eased the problems with organ rejection.

Jenkin's term of office was dominated by industrial action in the wider economy and the NHS and yet another messy and expensive reorganisation. It was a difficult two years spent mainly firefighting rather than building an improved NHS.

He went on to serve Mrs Thatcher at Industry where he introduced the first Bill privatising British Telecom and Environment before she asked him to stand down in 1985 to make way for new blood in the government.

In 1986 he was drawn into the Wessex RHA Computer scandal as an advisor to Arthur Anderson for whom he had been lobbying hard for the Wessex business.

He moved to the Lords as Baron Jenkin of Roding in 1987 and became an active member of the upper house.

From 1991-1997 he was Chair of the Forest Healthcare NHS Trust.

1926-2016

NORMAN FOWLER

September 1981-June 1987

Conservative

Norman Fowler was born in Essex and did his national service in the Essex Regiment. After his time at Cambridge University [where he had chaired the Conservative Association] he joined The Times as a journalist. He was part of the so-called Cambridge mafia who would climb the ranks of the Conservative Party over the next few decades.[118] In June 1970 he was elected MP for Nottingham South. He moved to the Sutton Coldfield constituency in 1974.

Margaret Thatcher appointed him a Minister of State for Transport in 1979 where he made seat belts compulsory, led on the decisions about the Channel Tunnel, rail electrification and the reform of the British Transport Docks Board. His post was upgraded to Secretary of State in January 1981.

In September 1981 he entered the Cabinet as Secretary of State for Health and Social Security. He remained in post for six years. His first team included Kenneth Clarke as his Minister of State. He had a reputation for being a cautious minister. As one colleague put it "Norman had a political mind that was almost Japanese. He looks at problems from all sides before making his mind up". He had always supported the principles of a National Health Service but as the pressure mounted on public expenditure, he thought it had to be made more efficient. You had to both correct the deficiencies of the past and keep up with the growth generated by medical science.

Shortly after he took up his post the NHS was reorganised. The Area tier was removed, and District Health Authorities took over as the main operational authorities. General Practitioners and the other independent contractors in primary care would be managed by Family Health Service Authorities who would report directly to the DHHS.

His first major challenge and what he called his baptism of fire was an industrial dispute about pay in the NHS which erupted at about the same time as the Falklands war. The public sector guideline for pay at the time was 4% but the independent Top Salaries Review Board had recommended huge rises for Judges [24%] and the recommendation for Doctors was 9%. He managed to get the award for doctors down to 6% which was the cause of much resentment. In June he increased the offer to nurses [7.5%] and to the ancillary and administrative and clerical staff to six percent. The offer was rejected, and industrial action began to intensify.[119],[120] Waiting lists began to rise. Everywhere that Fowler visited there were demonstrations, and some turned quite ugly. By this stage he had a police guard on his ministerial visits. A day of action in September 1982 brought about 60,000 people on to the streets of London. Having exhausted the normal negotiating channels Fowler made a

---

[118] Fowler, Howard, Gummer, Clarke, Brittan, Lamont and Lilly.
[119] Fowler estimates that 60,000 non-emergency operations had been cancelled by July of that year.
[120] The RCN initially accepted their offer and put it to a ballot of members who rejected it

direct and personal approach to the Union leaders which led to secret meetings at his house in Fulham. These meetings did not at the time produce a solution, but they did reopen a dialogue that had closed. A two-year deal was eventually settled in December 1982 which was widely regarded as a victory for the government. The nurses got a pay review body. Fowler was critical of the fact that he got little support from the management sides of the Whitley Councils or from Health Authorities.[121] It was largely this experience that persuaded him in 1983 to ask Roy Griffiths the Deputy Chair and Managing Director of Sainsbury's to review the management of the NHS. Kenneth Clarke his deputy was not enthusiastic about his appointment. A string of efficiency studies was launched including the sale of surplus land and unused staff accommodation and follow ups to the work of Sir Derek Rayner the Prime Ministers advisor on government efficiency. Manpower targets were set by ministers which impacted mainly on the non-clinical services in the NHS.

In September 1983 he instructed Health Authorities to competitively test the value for money they were getting from their ancillary services. Some authorities refused until it was made quite clear by Kenneth Clarke that if they objected, they could resign. They would certainly not be reappointed. Commercial companies did secure some contacts and over the years the reduction in ancillary staff headcount did yield savings of about £1 billion. However, the removal of housekeeping staff from the control of ward sisters was to prove a bad move.

In order to strengthen the accountability of health authorities, in 1982 he introduced an annual accountability review between ministers and regional health authorities. This proved to be a powerful tool in influencing both planning and operational decision making in the NHS. It was a challenging experience for Regional Chiefs to face ministers and account for their actions and performance, particularly as the follow up letter was made public. These reviews began to use the first set of performance indicators. In 1980/81 health authorities had been set efficiency targets which represented about 0.5% of total revenue spend.[122]

---

[121] In July 1982 he was kept waiting at a NAHAT conference whilst the members passed a motion condemning the government offer as divisive.

During the middle of the industrial relations dispute a highly controversial paper written by the Central Policy Review Staff was discussed in cabinet. It suggested that the government should consider moving away from a tax financed NHS to private health insurance. Fowler was opposed, mainly on practical grounds, and said so in cabinet. He had stopped some earlier internal work on alternative funding that had been commissioned by his predecessor Patrick Jenkin because he was sure that Margaret Thatcher was not up for major changes to the NHS at that time. The CPRS report was leaked which provided evidence for the Unions to claim that the government was intent on privatising the NHS. The controversy led to a firm rejection of the proposal at the party conference in October. "The NHS is safe with us "said Mrs Thatcher.[123]

Another controversial issue was the introduction of a limited list of drugs that could be prescribed by GPs.[124] The list excluded branded products for which there was a generic and cheaper alternative which was just as effective[125]. The BMA saw it as an attack on clinical freedom, but Fowler and Clarke stuck to their guns. Many clinicians agreed with them which sharply weakened the arguments of the BMA. In 1987 Fowler produced plans to improve general practice placing greater emphasis than before on prevention of illness and the promotion of health. It provided financial incentives for General Practitioners.[126]

He introduced charges for overseas visitors who used the NHS and in 1984 removed the optician's monopoly in supplying spectacles.

He also dealt with the problem of planning and funding those specialties that operated on a supra regional and national basis by setting up a special committee to undertake this task. The early list included the national poisons service, spinal injuries and the children's service for end stage renal failure. It would later include cardiac surgery for children which was to cause problems for some of his successors as they tried to limit the number of operating centres in the wake of the problems in Bristol.

---

[122] By 1983 this had evolved to locally worked up cost improvement programmes which had to be included in short term planning programmes.
[123] The genesis of this report was an in-house quick survey commissioned by Fowler but not published.
[124] Called a selective list by politicians and a limited list by doctor's leaders. Expected savings £75m.
[125] Alka Seltzer, Andrews Liver Salts, Vicks Vapour rub, Rock Salmon cough mixture.
[126] Cmd 249 Promoting Better Health.1987.

The Griffiths Report became available in the middle of 1983 with a vivid headline; "If Florence Nightingale was carrying her lamp through the corridors of the NHS today, she would be searching for the people in charge"[127]. He advised the creation of a new core of general managers who would take responsibility for securing the best service for patients and who could be held to account if there was a failure. At the Department of Health, a new NHS Management Board would report to an NHS Supervisory Board chaired by the Secretary of State. The BMA and the health professions were very suspicious of the introduction of business management into the NHS, but Fowler was determined to proceed. Another reorganisation was launched as people from all disciplines applied for the new jobs as general managers. Most where filled by former Administrators. Victor Paige who Fowler had worked with at Transport [He had been Chair of the Port of London Authority] was appointed as the first chair of the NHS Management Board. The CMO reluctantly joined the NHS Management Board but after some serious thought. He had wider responsibilities than the NHS and did not want to become accountable to Victor Paige.

Paige only lasted eighteen months when he resigned because of a lack of clarity about his role and authority. He later explained that "One of the reasons for the confusion relates to the decision to appoint the Chairman as a second permanent secretary. I was not aware of the reasoning behind that, but I believe it was cultivated by the civil service moguls who perhaps would have wished to retain the chairmanship of this unusual body within the civil service".[128]

Fowler had made it clear that "officials advise, and Ministers decide".

Ken Stowe put it bluntly as follows;" There are volumes of history on how best to operate the operational and policy functions in respect of health authorities. The only principle that matters is that all officials have a single accountability to the Secretary of State. There are no representatives of the NHS in the Department. The objective of Griffiths was to permit a high ranking official to give all his time to the management of health authorities, supported by others

---

[127] The phrase is attributed to Cliff Graham the civil servant who supported Roy Griffiths.
[128] Edwards and Fall. The Executive years of the NHS.

who were similarly dedicated, without being preoccupied as I and others were with policy issues." [129]

Len Peach the Director of Human Resources for the NHS [on secondment from IBM] became chairman on a temporary basis as Ministers considered what to do. A few months later in November 1986 Tony Newton the Minister of State took over the Chair of the NHS Management Board as a means of reasserting ministerial authority. His deputy was Roy Griffiths and Len Peach became Chief Executive of the NHS. Peach was judged to have a flair for multidisciplinary management and did not need the clarity about his personal powers that Paige had sought. The management board began to talk about a corporate identity for the whole NHS. They clearly saw themselves as being in charge of the whole system in England. They also began to have monthly meetings with the chief executives of regional health authorities. They began to get deeply involved in NHS day to day operations.

The Supervisory Board which was supposed to be at the top of the Department of Health did not prove to be a success despite some distinguished members. It had in the view of Victor Paige been designed to keep Ministers and the Permanent Secretary out of the Management Board. It never had a decision-making role and was at best a group of advisors sitting around the Secretary of State's table acting as his sounding board. It was wound up by Kenneth Clarke in 1989.

It was Aids that dominated the public health agenda and Fowler acted forcefully and decisively. Aids had been isolated and characterised in 1983 but its incidence began to accelerate in 1987 with 281 cases in the first six months. His solution was a mass education campaign that talked directly about the association with sexual intercourse and homosexuality." Don't die of ignorance" was one of the major themes. £14 million was invested in the search for a vaccine.

In 1984 nineteen patients died of salmonella at Stanley Royd Hospital in Wakefield which led to a public inquiry. One consequence was an Inquiry led by the CMO Donald Acheson into the future role of public health and the other was the removal of crown immunity from the NHS.

---

[129] Edwards and Fall.

In 1986 Fowler re-opened the policy debate about the future of community care by asking Roy Griffiths to undertake a further review. The discussions and arguments would go on for another 40 years. Social care was an expensive business.

Changes to the structures for regulating nurses had been rumbling slowly on since the Briggs Report in 1972.In 1986 the Project 2000 report was published recommending a common foundation programme for nurse education, a specialist register and that student nurses should be supernumerary to NHS staffing establishments. The Cumberledge Report on community nursing had been published in October 1986 recommending neighbourhood nursing teams rather than attachment to general practice. General Practitioners objected strongly. A new nurse grading system was proving difficult to implement and would lead to appeals for years to come.

Behind the scenes debates about the future direction of the NHS continued. In January 1987 Ken Stowe the permanent secretary had laid out a case for change. The paper reviewed private health insurance, patient charges [hotel costs et al], an independent NHS Corporation and the practicalities of introducing competition on the lines advocated by Alain Enthoven an American guru. The paper was discussed with Margaret Thatcher in January 1987, but no conclusions were reached. The discussions were, she recorded in her memoirs, very theoretical. The time was not right she judged for significant changes to the principles of the NHS.

Fowler always claimed to have "all-star" ministerial teams which included political heavyweights such as John Major [in social security], Kenneth Clarke and Tony Newton and newsworthy ministers like Edwina Currie. Very unusually he worked with the same permanent secretary Kenneth Stowe for almost all his six years. They forged a very strong partnership. Stowe recalls "Norman Fowler and I had a very, very good relationship in which we absolutely trusted each other. He knew that I would be thinking about how to do this…. I had no inhibitions about carrying my thinking forward as far as I could and then going back to him and saying…. this might be a way to do it."

In 1987 Fowler moved to become Employment Secretary. He resigned to spend more time with his family in 1990 but returned in 1992 as Chairman of the Conservative Party and later a series of opposition spokesman posts.

He retired as an MP in 2001 and entered the Lords as Baron Fowler of Sutton Coldfield. He played an active role in the House of Lords and became Lord Speaker in 2016. He chaired a Lords committee on the continued spread of Aids in 2011.

Much had happened during Fowler's long term of office in health. The NHS had become marginally more efficient and a management ethos had been injected into a complex area of the public sector. The centre had tightened its grip on the management of the NHS. His vigorous action on Aids was widely respected. His resolute response to industrial action sets a precedent for future conflicts during the Thatcher government. Mrs Thatcher regarded him as a very good defensive player.

1938-date

JOHN MOORE

July 1987-July 1988

John Moore was born in London and after leaving school did his national service in Korea. He read for a degree at LSE where he was active in student politics. He then moved to the USA where he worked for banks and stockbroking firms. He got involved in American politics and was an activist for the Democratic Party in Illinois. In 1968 he returned to London as Chairman of

Dean Witter International the company he had worked for in Chicago. He served as a Councillor in Merton before securing the Central Croydon seat in 1974. He was described by a colleague as "handsome, personable and polite and looking ten years younger than he actually was". His wife was heavily involved in his political life. In 1979 as Under Secretary of State for Energy he had responsibility for the privatisation of the coal industry. When he moved to the Treasury in 1983, he led on privatisation including the sale of British Telecom. He joined Margaret Thatcher's Cabinet in 1986 as Secretary of State for Transport where he presided over the opening of the M25 and the privatisation of British Airways.

As one observer put it "In this job the script had been written for him, he had only to learn the lines." He came to be regarded as an implementer of policy rather than a great thinker.

He became Secretary of State for Social Services at a time when the NHS was in the middle of yet another financial crisis. The NHS was according to Ian Mills it's Director of Finance technically bankrupt. The NHS was told that it could not overspend, and so beds began to close, recruitment was suspended, and Treasurers began to slow down the payment of bills. Moore blamed Fowler. Despite his strong public image, he was not a popular minister. Edwina Currie thought him weak and not up to the job. John Major when Chancellor of the Exchequer was reported to have found him a soft touch in negotiations about NHS funding. By some accounts he wanted to burnish his political credentials by not asking for more money for the NHS.

Shortly after taking office Moore had received a report on medical staffing called Achieving a Balance. It was a joint effort between the Department of Health and the Joint Consultant's Committee. The number of Consultants was set to rise steadily over the next ten years and the number of junior staffs in training linked to this number. [130]200 new posts were injected into the pot from central funds and it was agreed that a new sub Consultant grade be created. This was quite an important step as the BMA had been resisting any expansion of doctor numbers for some time.

---

[130] The increase would be around 2% a year.

He reshaped the NHS Policy Board to provide a small forum to consider major issues. He appears to have had a problem building close working relationships with civil servants and some attribute this to his wife who was also his political advisor. He ran into heavy politics in Birmingham in November 1987 when the media got their teeth into a story about a baby at Birmingham Children's Hospital with a hole in the heart who had had his operation cancelled 5 times because of a shortage of intensive care nurses.[131] A week or two later Moore was struck down with pneumonia and was absent from government for two months. He blamed his illness in part on the offices at the Elephant and Castle and was much relieved by the move to Whitehall later that year.[132] He chose to be treated at a private hospital which caused much critical comment. Tony Newton took over in his absence and managed to persuade the Treasury to inject £101m into the NHS to relieve the short-term pressure. It was not enough to satisfy the Presidents of the medical royal colleges who told the Prime Minister that she had to act now to save the NHS. In January 1988 Moore, now back at his desk, was badly mauled in the Commons about NHS funding. Six days later Margaret Thatcher announced her review of the NHS. It would be conducted by four ministers [Moore, Newton, Lawson and Major] and herself. Moore argued for an insurance-based system. He wanted to make private health insurance contributions tax deductible. He got little support from the rest of the review team.

NHS pay was a constant issue during his term of office. The trade unions organising a national day of protest in February 1988. The protesters included many nurses who were members of NUPE. A South Yorkshire pit was brought to a standstill when 200 miners refused to cross a nurse's picket line at the colliery gate. Nurses had been offered a 3% rise and local pay bargaining which he strongly supported. Two months later they secured a 15% award and retained national bargaining

In May 1988 he accepted the broad thrust of the Project 2000 report on nurse education which resulted in schools of nursing moving into the university sector. Nurses in training would become proper students with a non-means

---

[131] Edwina Curry Diaries 1987-1992. Little Brown. 2002.
[132] Richmond House opposite Downing Street.

tested bursary. The Enrolled Nurse was to be phased out. Almost certainly to his surprise he got a standing ovation at the RCN conference that year.

The NHS review was making little progress when in July 1988 the DHHS was split into two. Kenneth Clarke took over health and Moore retained social security. He lost his Cabinet seat in 1989 and left the House of Commons at the general election in 1992 and moved to the Lords as Baron Moore of Lower Marsh. It took him 20 years to make his maiden speech in the Lords.

Moore was only in post for twelve months and ill for two of those. He had his admirers as a good political operator and had been regarded as a potential party leader. His rise had been meteoritic under Margaret Thatcher, but most regarded him as a weak minister with a poor touch for British politics. Don Wilson the leading regional chair explained "I cannot get close to him; cannot figure him out"

1937-date

KENNETH CLARKE

July 1988-November 1990

Conservative

Kenneth Clarke was born in Nottinghamshire. He read law at Cambridge where he was also Chair of the University Conservative Association. He was a member of the Cambridge political mafia as was his former boss Norman Fowler. He was called to the Bar in 1963 and appointed a Queen's Council in 1980.

He started to search for a seat in the House of Commons almost immediately after leaving university and in June 1970 at the age of 29 he was elected in Rushcliffe south of Nottingham. Since his election to Parliament he has served four Prime Ministers in almost all the most senior posts in Government. He has always been a strong advocate of membership of the EU. He stood, unsuccessfully, for election as party leader on three occasions. He comes from the liberal end of the Conservative Party and once told a Conservative conference that "our society must not only be efficient but must also be humane, just and compassionate."

Clarke's first appointment in Health was Minister of State under Norman Fowler. They waded energetically into the problem of making the NHS more efficient. They insisted that NHS ancillary services be tested against external competition, that generic drugs were prescribed when appropriate and unused staff accommodation be sold off. Fowler appointed Roy Griffiths to review NHS management and despite his reservations about the whole idea Clarke played a significant role in first finding and then appointing Victor Paige as the first Chair of the NHS Management Board the forerunner to Chief Executive of the NHS. Paige led the introduction of general management into the NHS.

Clarke returned to Health in 1988 when the DHHS was broken up. On appointment he found the Thatcher review of the NHS well underway but not getting very far. He fought hard against the introduction of an insurance-based system and tax reliefs and claimed the credit for introducing GP Fund Holding. The NHS had to be more business-like he argued. Nobody in the NHS had any idea what they spent public money on he told his colleagues. Clarke warned the Cabinet that when the reform package was announced there would be "a hell of a row". None seemed unduly perturbed by this including Margaret Thatcher now at the height of her powers.

The reform package was launched by Clarke on 31st January 1989 at the Limehouse in London which was linked to teleconferencing venues in the provinces. By his side was the new Chief Executive of the NHS Duncan Nichol. This was a prime example of Clarke's interest in the effective communication of policies and ideas both within the NHS and the wider media. Nichol had been appointed despite Margaret Thatcher's preference for another manager.[133] Clarke was determined to have his choice in post.

The reform package created an internal market within the NHS. The money would follow the patients. Those engaged in commissioning treatment for NHS

---

[133] Chris West. Portsmouth.

patients would be separated from those who provided it. GP Fundholding would drive innovation. NHS Trusts would have substantial freedoms to manage their own affairs. Consultants would have tighter job descriptions. The private sector would be encouraged to provide clinical services to NHS patients but only at the margins. The NHS would remain a state funded service free to all at the point of need. However, the balance of power within the system would swing away from hospitals and their consultants to primary care and General Practitioners.[134] It was set up with the simple aim "Do more, better"[135]

There was a sceptical silence within the NHS as people tried to work out how it would all operate. The BMA claim to have held back on immediate comment whilst they sought more detail[136]. The detail was not yet there only the outline could be seen. According to the BMA negotiators this did not stop Clarke accusing them of always objecting to change. The next few months saw the publication of a series of working papers which filled in much of the detail.[137] The reform package turned out to be much more extensive than people had at first appreciated. Consultant contracts would be switched to local employers and managers would be involved in Consultant selection committees and on the committees that decided who would receive medical merit awards. The BMA argued with some force that breaking the principle that all Consultants wherever they worked in the NHS were paid the same would halt the spread of specialist expertise. Their arguments fell on deaf ears. Some years later Clarke was to reflect somewhat ruefully that if he had not challenged national pay bargaining for doctors, he might have minimised the medical opposition to the wider reform programme.[138] Consultant pay has always been a significant national issue.

Clinical audit would become compulsory. Indicative prescribing budgets would be introduced into general practice. As a sop to the doctors 100 new consultant appointments would be authorised. Health Authorities would be slimmed down and become more executive. Local authorities would no longer have specified seats on NHS Boards. A new Policy Board chaired by the

---

[134] GP Fundholding was initially restricted to practices with over 11,000 patients
[135] Eric Caines former Director of Personnel. NHS Executive. BMJ 1994.308 455.
[136] A Damn Bad Business. The NHS Deformed. J. Lee Potter. Gollancz 1997
[137] There were eleven working papers in the end.
[138] The Greatest Experiment. Nuffield Trust .2008.

Secretary of State would oversee the work of an NHS Executive chaired by Duncan Nichol. The Nichol Executive was made up predominantly of senior civil servants with Graham Hart a future Permanent Secretary as his deputy. The Policy Board included the ministerial team [Mellor, Freeman, Hooper], the Permanent Secretary [France] and CMO [Acheson] as well as the Chairs of British Steel [Scholey], British Aerospace [Durham], The Rover Group [Day], two regional chairs [Cumberlege and Ackers]and Cyril Chantler a Consultant from Guy's Hospital. Sir Roy Griffiths was deputy chair. Duncan Nichol was also a member.

As the scale of the planned changes began to emerge the opposition mounted.

The NHS was the BMA said "underfunded, undermined and under threat". Clarke rebuffed their demands for a pilot scheme claiming they would sabotage it. The BMA then ran a major national publicity campaign which included a striking poster which said *"What do you call a man who ignores medical advice. Mr Clarke"*.

Managers who wanted their units to operate as NHS Trusts had to first earn this status by demonstrating their financial health and robust leadership. For some it was a passage of fire with their local communities and MPs. Clarke could have simply rebadged existing organisations, but he chose instead to make them apply for promised new freedoms. The BMA tried to get local Consultants to block applications but failed. In regions such as Trent which had amongst the highest number of bids, applications only went forward if local managers secured the support of their local doctors. Many Consultants quite liked the idea that their hospital would have substantial freedoms and some new revenue streams. Many GP's were excited about fundholding particularly as the change was to be evolutionary.

A lot of energy was put into working up a set of rules for the NHS internal market. It was a not to be a free for all. It was designed to generate efficiency not profit.

Whilst the changes involved a major reorganisation of the NHS, they were not the centre piece of the change programme. The most powerful change was the introduction of the internal market. New Boards had a more business-like make up with Board level Directors and Non-Executive Directors who for the first time were paid a modest stipend.[139] 90 Family Health Service Authorities would manage GPs and the other independent contractor services working alongside 190 District Health Authorities. Both would be accountable to 14 Regional Health Authorities.

Throughout the preparations for introducing the internal market Clarke had to cope with constant pressure from Downing Street where Mrs Thatcher and her advisors were anxious about progress. This led to several heated arguments between Clarke and Thatcher. Clarke persevered and kept going as the NHS Bill worked its way through Parliament. The internal market went live on 1st April 1991 with a relatively smooth and controlled take off. In part this was due to the elimination of all[most] underlying deficits before the market went live.

Running alongside the reform programme was a negotiation about GP contracts which would extend capitation funding and insert financial incentives for preventative activities. Clarke probably made a strategic error by commenting at a Royal College dinner that "I do wish that the more suspicious of our GPs would stop feeling nervously for their wallets every time I mention the word reform". The leaders of the profession were furious. In the end Clarke reached a deal with the BMA negotiators only to have it rejected by doctors in a national ballot. A new contract was eventually enforced. It was not a bad settlement at all although many GPs still blame the 1990 contract for demoralising general practice. The new deal might have been designed to lift standards, but GP leaders were not convinced that a new contract was what the profession needed. It was, some thought, an unwelcome intrusion into their professional freedoms and integrity.

In Autumn 1990 Clarke reflected on this experience in a piece for the BMJ" I have quite a reputation with doctors for being extremely and belligerently inflexible. My defence is that I am doing something that is not with the consent of the community of doctors and the BMA. They are accustomed to telling the government what their opinion is and expect the government to do as they are told".

---

[139] The largest single business interest of the new Non-Executive Directors was property development.

He lost Edwina Currie one of his junior ministers in 1988 following a problem with salmonella in eggs. He did not seem overly concerned.

In the summer of 1989 Ambulance crews who wanted parity with the fire service introduced a ban on overtime and rest day working. The army were put on standby. Clarke was as robust as usual "Of all the things you can spend money on in the NHS, buying off strikes is the worst". The dispute was eventually settled twenty-four weeks later with an eighteen month pay deal worth 17.6%...but no parity. Both sides claimed victory. [140]Clarke encouraged Duncan Nichol to play a major and public role in managing the dispute, but he kept being dragged in by Parliament and the media. To create distance between himself and the NHS Executive and give them some organisational space he moved the NHS Executive to Leeds in his last days in office.[141]

It was Clarke who first decided to include clinical outcomes in the performance management of health authorities a foundation which would allow his successors to launch the Health of the Nation.

The Roy Griffiths report on community care came out in 1988 but the government response was delayed for a year because of the potential cost[142]. Local authorities were to emerge as commissioners of care services rather than direct providers of care. There was to be a major transfer of funds from social security to local government.

The winter of 1989/90 saw a very severe influenza outbreak which resulted in 25,000 deaths in England and Wales. It put enormous pressure on the NHS but attracted very little media attention.[143]Concern about the possible spread of mad cow disease did however capture the headlines but action was left to John Gummer in Agriculture.

Kenneth Clarke was not a popular minister in the professional ranks of the Department of Health. He had a healthy disrespect for experts when they offered opinion rather than evidence. He did earn the respect of many NHS managers for his willingness to confront challenging issues. He worked well

---

[140] One side effect of the dispute was an acceleration of paramedic training.
[141] The NHS Executive moved to Leeds in July 1992.They kept an office in Whitehall.
[142] Some of his recommendations were finally implemented in 1993.
[143] On the State of the Public Health 1989.

with Duncan Nichol the Chief Executive of the NHS who led the preparations for the introduction of the internal market. Nichol and France the Permanent Secretary sorted out their respective roles quite quickly. Margaret Thatcher had made it plain that she wanted Nichol to act as a Chief Executive rather than a civil service advisor to ministers.[144]

In a cabinet reshuffle in the final weeks of the Thatcher government Clarke was moved, to his surprise, to Science and Education. He had been in office at Health for only 28 months and his reforms did not start until the following April when he would not be there. He would later become Home Secretary and Chancellor of the Exchequer. In this latter role he gave his successors at health a hard time.

It is undoubtedly true that no other politician in his generation could have driven through such an extensive reform programme. It is unlikely that it could have got through with reasoned argument and debate. Although Frank Dobson promised to abolish the internal market the Blair government accepted the broad thrust of Clarke's reforms and developed some of them further in the NHS Plan that was to come. Whether market forces can grow healthy and thriving health systems remains a deeply contentious issue. There were many industrial disputes in which Clarke gained his reputation as a tough minister willing to take on those who got in his way. A battle was never personal and some of his Trade Union opponents would later talk about his human face. Margaret Thatcher admired his toughness and his communication skills, but they never became close. She regarded him "as an energetic and persuasive bruiser, very useful in a brawl or an election". A columnist in the BMJ marked his departure from Health "with a grudging respect only normally found between opposing armies on the field of war".

He certainly changed the NHS.

In his later parliamentary career, he stuck firmly to his pro-European guns.

---

[144] The Executive Years of the NHS, Edwards and Fall. Nuffield Trust .2005.

WILLIAM WALDEGRAVE

November 1990-April 1992

Conservative

William Waldegrave came from an aristocratic family and was educated at Eton where in later years he became Provost. He studied at Oxford where he became a Fellow of All Souls College. He was recruited from Harvard University by Rothschild to join the Central Policy Review Staff and later served in Edward Heath's private office. He was elected MP for Bristol West in 1979. He held several junior posts before becoming a Minister of State at Environment and then the Foreign Office. He was appointed to the Cabinet as Secretary of State for Health by Margaret Thatcher just shortly before she resigned. He continued under John Major. Mrs Thatcher described him as slim, cerebral and aloof. Virginia Bottomley continued in office as his Minister of State.

He found himself implementing the internal market in the NHS with Duncan Nichol the NHS Chief Executive and with a significant increase in revenue that had been negotiated by Kenneth Clark[145]. He brought a quieter and softer language to the process of change in the NHS. He wanted a smooth, quiet take off for the internal market. The BMA welcomed him warmly and hoped for some changes to the Clarke reforms. He was, they judged, a thinker rather than a politician.[146] The BMA liked the way in which he listened to their arguments but were taken aback somewhat when he approved the applications from 57 hospitals to become NHS Trusts in the first wave. 306 GP Fund Holding Practice approvals was to follow. Waldegrave may have softened the language but the reforms continued. He told the Tory party Central Committee in March 1991 "The NHS embodies an ideal, but this does not mean that we should not subject it's ramshackle structures, jerry built in the 1940's and clad in concrete in the 1960's, to the most vigorous appraisal". He gave no ground at all on the principle of introducing competition into the NHS and accepted Treasury demands for efficiency targets.

---

[145] NHS spending rose by £3billion in 1990-91 and by almost as much again in 1991-2.
[146] A Damn Bad Business. J. Lee Potter. 1997

In March 1991 he made it plain to the Chairmen of Regional Health Authorities in what became known as the "Waldegrave Letter"[147] that NHS Trusts would be accountable "to me and my successors as Secretary of State". He gave all first wave Trust chairs his personal telephone number to ring if they had problems. The Trusts loved him for it. By the end of 1991 most NHS providers had expressed an interest in becoming NHS Trusts. This was not always easy as Robin Cook the opposition spokesman had made it plain to those managers who were leading bids for Trust status in Labour heartlands that they would have no personal future in the NHS should Labour return to office. This was straightforward intimidation, but it had little impact.

The nurses liked him as he added the name of Anne Poole the Chief Nursing Officer to the NHS Policy Board alongside Peter Gummer and Jean Denton both experts in public relations.

The internal market went live on 1st April 1991. It flushed out into the open enormous variations in price for common procedures which was pretty much what was intended. Despite the expected teething problems, the NHS adjusted quickly to the internal market. The enthusiasm of many GP Fundholders and doctors in NHS Trusts took much of the sting out of the continued opposition by the BMA. John Major added his weight as Prime Minister to the defence of the new NHS by declaring that "there would be no privatisation of health care, neither piecemeal nor in part, nor in whole, not today or tomorrow, not after the next election, not ever whilst I am Prime Minister"

Waldegrave launched yet another attempt to sort out the NHS in London. He knew he had problems because so many of London's major hospitals were failing the test to become NHS Trusts. Although he was accused of "wringing his hands over London" he made it clear that any decisions had to have a sound intellectual foundation. He appointed Professor Bernard Tomlinson to undertake a review on the advice of Virginia Bottomley who knew him well as a Regional Chair.[148] It would he said, "force some decisions out of us cowardly politicians who for twenty years have put them off". He had moved on by the time Tomlinson reported.

---

[147] 6/3/1991.
[148] He was a doctor from Newcastle but trained in London

Perhaps his most notable achievement was the work he encouraged on "The Health of the Nation". In June 1991 he published a consultative paper outlining proposals for a strategic approach to health policy. In it he acknowledged that the NHS could not solve all the country's health problems; life style, environment and socio-economic factors were also important. With John Major he organised a major meeting at Chequers to flesh out the policy with the leaders of the health professions and the NHS. This led to a White paper in July 1992. Included in the targets was Equity in Health which demanded a reduction in the disparity in health status between different groups within the population. The clinical priorities embedded in Health of the Nation and the targets for health gain started to reshape the managerial challenge in the NHS.

It was during his term of office that the Patient's Charter was launched in 1991 which laid down standards and guarantees for patients including a maximum two year wait for non-emergency surgery. There was also a national research and development plan. [149]In June 1991 Waldegrave struck a New Deal with the doctors which rationalised working time and resulted in 200 extra consultants and 50 new staff grade posts. He continued to press for waiting time reductions and by March 1992 the number of patients waiting longer than two years had come down to just under 2000.

Waldegrave was liked by his civil servants and he built an effective relationship with the health professions and with Duncan Nichol and his NHS Executive. He was, the Chairman of the BMA said, "well informed, unusually frank and open for a politician and had an instinctive compatibility with doctors". He mistrusted large bureaucracies and regarded the principle that Ministers were accountable to Parliament for everything that happened in their Departments as nonsense. Waldegrave was a big picture politician.

In the autumn of 1991 Waldegrave [and John Major] found themselves having to defend Duncan Nichol who had at Waldegrave's request given an interview to the Daily Mail in which he made it plain that there was not a shred of evidence that the government was intent on privatising the NHS. Robin Cook was furious and complained to the head of the civil service. Waldegrave was clear that whilst civil servants had to act like chameleons, managers had to

---

[149] Michael Peckham was the first Director of Research and Development.

commit to and own a management plan. The role of managers in Whitehall would continue to present problems for years to come. Nichol knew that should Labour win the next general election his chances of remaining in office were slim.

Waldegrave has since argued that the NHS is not the only way of delivering a national health care system. Somehow he explained "you have to separate out a national commitment to fairness where there are not people who can't get proper care and the commitment to the great, huge sort of grumbling organisational structure of the NHS"[150] The NHS Executive who now produced their own annual report expressed it rather differently "We are the largest employer in Europe with a workforce of over 850, 000, a turnover in excess of £26 billion and a service commitment to 47 million people. We share one aim…to create a better health service for the nation.[151]

In April 1992 Waldegrave moved to the Cabinet Office with responsibility for public services and science. He was heavily involved in the Citizens Charter and in science offered a prize for best explanation of Higgs Boson.

He was only in office at Health for eighteen months. Although some doubted his taste for political infighting, his intellectual rigor and honesty would have served the NHS well had he continued in office.

He lost his seat at the 1997 election and joined the House of Lords as Baron Waldegrave of North Hill.

1946-Date

---

[150] Rejuvenate or Retire. Views of the NHS at 60. Nuffield Trust.
[151] NHS Executive Report November 1992.

Virginia Bottomley

April 1992- July 1995

Conservative

Virginia Bottomley was the daughter of John Garnett who was the Director of the Industrial Society between 1986-90. He was also Chair of the West Lambeth Health Authority which included St Thomas's Hospital. She was educated at Essex University and the LSE. Her whole family were engaged in London politics. She became a social worker and magistrate before she secured her seat in Parliament in 1984. She was on the left of her party and regarded herself as a public servant.

After a series of junior ministerial posts, she joined Ken Clarke's team at the Department of Health in 1989 as he was battling through his reforms to the NHS. She continued as a Minister of State when William Waldegrave took over. She gained a reputation as a hard-working minister but not one with strongly expressed political passions. She liked to circle difficult decisions and take extensive soundings before reaching a decision. For her officials this was a mixed blessing.

The 1992 election campaign placed the NHS at the centre of fierce political debate. The "war of Jennifer's ear" had broken out when the Labour Party named a five-year-old who had waited over a year for treatment to her glue ear. This was contrary to the Broadcast rules according to the Conservatives.[152]Labour was still fighting the Clarke reforms.

Bottomley's elevation to Secretary of State by John Major in 1992 came as a pleasant surprise. She had Brian Mawhinney a political bruiser from Northern Ireland as her Minister of State [Health]. Her job was to continue the lead of

---

[152] The headline is an illusion to the war of Jenkins' ear in the eighteenth century

William Waldegrave in bedding down the internal market in the NHS and wipe away its sharper edges with what John Major described as her steely grace. She was, Major thought, relentless, courageous and magnificent.[153] If Ken Clarke had been the window breaker, she was the glazier. She preferred light touch to soviet style command and control. She encouraged Duncan Nichol to get on with managing the NHS and as far as was possible turned a deaf ear to the sound of Bevan's dropped bed pans.[154] She understood the health brief very well having been the Minister of State for three years prior to her appointment as Secretary of State.

Shortly after she had taken office ministers began to talk again about the problems, they [and Duncan Nichol] were having with a few of the NHS Regions and their chairs who had become very powerful and demanded direct access to Ministers. Whilst some Regions were pressing on with creating the internal market, encouraging Trusts and Fundholding, others were dragging their feet. To stimulate the Trust movement [and bypass the Regions] applications for Trust status were made direct to the Department of Health Trust Unit who eventually developed regional outposts. Regional Health Authorities were told to focus their energies on supporting the new commissioners and cut their staff. The Trust Federation having seen their members escape regional oversight did not want to see their freedoms curbed and said so vociferously. The Trusts rather liked their direct link to the Department of Health and the Secretary of State and wanted this relationship to continue. At a meeting at Chevening in July 1992 Ministers concluded that whilst some intermediate tier was essential to provide a strategic bridge between commissioners of NHS care and NHS Trusts, the RHAs could be reduced in number [14 to 8] and eventually replaced by regional offices of the NHS Executive. The plan to move to eight was sorted out by Duncan Nichol and Brian Mawhinney in an Indian restaurant in Cambridge. The final decision was announced by Bottomley in October 1994. This was an uncomfortable conclusion for Bottomley as she valued the support of Regional Chairs who liked to think of themselves as her NHS kitchen cabinet. She decided to keep them as her representative in the regions where they acted as her eyes and ears. However, once they lost their power base their influence faded, and their

---

[153] John Major. The Autobiography. Harper Collins 1999.
[154] Timmins. A Biography of the Welfare State. Harper Collins 1995.

role became limited to the search for new non-executive members for health Boards. Eight of them joined her policy board. The Regional Chief Executives and their staff were assimilated into Duncan Nichol's NHS Executive.

Bottomley's attitude to the Regions would have been deeply influenced by the problems in Wessex, West Midlands and Yorkshire all of whom found themselves in front of the Public Accounts Committee to explain and justify problems in their regions and at their headquarters. Improper early retirement deals were also under scrutiny by the National Audit office.[155] In their enthusiasm to become more business-like some regions had stepped over public sector probity lines. But the regions were not her only restructuring venture as in December 1993 it was announced that District Health Authorities and Family Health Service Authorities would merge.

Working arrangements between the NHS and Local Government became particularly important when it came to implement the community care reforms in 1993. Bottomley secured a one-off transitional grant. As the changes in social care began to bite and she insisted that local authorities spent at least 85% of the earmarked cash provided from central government in the independent sector. Councils were to be commissioners of care not providers. Old people's homes managed by Local Authorities began to be phased out.

Smoking remained the biggest public health challenge as 28% of adults in England were regular smokers. In March 1994 the Scientific Committee on Smoking and Health was set up to report directly to Kenneth Calman the CMO. They recommended that the prime focus for action should switch to young people.

Bottomley worked hard building a new relationship with the health professions and on one occasion got a standing ovation from the BMA. In 1993 she accepted the Calman Report on Medical Training which led to new ways of training specialists. She pushed health authorities to improve the working and living conditions for junior doctors.

---

[155] The Venning's Trawl

The doctors rather liked her as a person but in private had doubts about whether she had the steel and the vision to handle the difficult policy decisions that were beginning to emerge.[156]

She pushed hard for action on the Patients Charter[157] and encouraged the early thinking inside the Department about the measurement and improvement in the quality of the patient experience. She perhaps more than her predecessors had an instinctive identification with the interests of patients.

The Allitt report on the murder of children at Grantham hospital was a poignant reminder of patient danger.[158]

The Health of the Nation policy initiative continued to be a centre piece for the Chief Medical Officer and the policy division inside the Department. Whilst the policy had been widely supported, she did get some caustic comment from her fellow parliamentarians who sometimes referred to her, very unfairly, as Nanny Bottomley. [159]

She encouraged purchasers/commissioners to reflect Health of the Nation targets in local contract negotiations, but this policy was still at the edges of the day to day life of managers in the field. They were focused on the problems of today and this hid a deeper and long-standing policy dilemma. Could you separate out policy and implementation? Could the NHS Executive [now based in Leeds][160] be limited to implementing policy once it had been settled by Ministers and civil servants? The battle raged within the headquarters until it was finally settled in 1994 with the Banks Report. Policy [or at least the bulk of it] and implementation were to be combined under the NHS Executive. Integrated working was to be the watchword as Kenneth Clarke now Chancellor of the Exchequer demanded a 21% cut in headquarters costs[161]. One of the principal casualties of integrated working was the CMO who found his personal empire sharply reduced. People from the NHS began to dominate

---

[156] A Damn Bad Business. J Lee Potter. Gollancz 1997.
[157] She asked Brian Edwards the Chief Executive from Trent RHA to lead on Charter implementation.
[158] 1994.
[159] HSJ 60th Anniversary Supplement.3/8/08.
[160] The NHS Executive at this stage included the eight regional directors amongst its members as well as headquarters staff.
[161] The regional offices were limited to 200 people.

the Department of Health and held more of the most senior posts than career civil servants.

Bottomley pushed District Health Authorities and GP Fund Holders to up their game in purchasing services for NHS patients. She asked Brian Mawhinney her Minister of State to work on this with Duncan Nichol. One case "Child B" [162] caused her and officials a good deal of heart searching. Cambridgeshire Health Authority had in March 1995 declined to pay, on good medical advice, for experimental treatment to a young child with cancer. The father challenged the decision in the High Court and lost. The press took up the case and offered to pay. Bottomley took the view that as the Health Authority had taken proper advice they should be supported. Care she said must be cost effective[163]. She did not like people talking about the rationing; it was priority setting!

She had been in office for more than two years when the Department issued its guide to the internal market which was designed as a guide rather than a restraint on health organisations. It was however a managed market not a free for all. The NHS would remain in the public sector with its traditional probity values and rules. The guide tried hard to distinguish between local freedoms and national responsibilities.[164] None of this arrested the growth in national targets and guidance. She lowered the threshold for entry to GP Fundholding to 5000 patients.

The NHS was not a business she told the Royal Society of Medicine in 1995 "the only profit it makes is measured in the cure of illness, the care of the sick, the relief of pain and its contribution to a healthier nation. We are all its shareholders; but our interest is human, not financial."

The NHS may not have been a business but that did not stop the Treasury pressing for higher and higher efficiency targets.5% they thought ought to be achievable![165] By 1993/4 NHS funding had dropped like a stone from the 7% growth in the previous year to less than 1%.Bottomley fought hard and secured a good result in 1994/5 with 4.1% but it fell back again to 1.6% in

---

[162] Later identified as Jaymee Bowen.
[163] The child eventually had the treatment but died shortly afterwards.
[164] The Operation of the Internal market. December 1994
[165] Clive Smee. Speaking Truth to Power. Nuffield Trust 2005.

1995/6 and 0.5% in the run up to the 1997 election.[166] The arguments opened up again about alternative funding sources, but Bottomley was not interested.

As a London MP she could not help but get involved in the politics of the NHS in London. The Tomlinson Report came onto her desk in October 1992 and as expected provoked a major public row. He had recommended a radical upgrading of primary care in the capital and a rationalisation of the hospital sector. There would have to be some mergers and several world class specialist hospitals [including Bart's] would have to be integrated[merged] into some of their larger neighbours. She sent it out for consultation and then created the London Implementation Group to coordinate the planning work of the four regions.[167] They launched a series of specialty reviews to build on the Tomlinson recommendations. Bottomley emerged from this process having made modest progress but more than a few enemies. Even the Kings Fund at one stage had described her plans for London as flawed. The Health Service Journal view of Mrs Bottomley upholding her family traditions of marching towards gunfire in her determination to tackle the London problem would be a lasting one. She made more progress sorting out medical education in the capital. One of the spin offs from the work in London was the specialty reviews and associated plans for hospital rationalisation that began to take place in other major cities.

In 1994 Duncan Nichol decided to retire as Chief Executive and Alan Langlands was appointed in his place. Bottomley was not involved in the interview process. The Cabinet Secretary was however as this was a post graded as a permanent secretary. Behind the scenes she would have seen and almost certainly approved the short list[168]. Interestingly Roy Griffiths now the Prime Minister's special advisor on health service management was excluded. Langlands understood from the start that his was not a classic chief executive role in the commercial mode. He was an administrator working to politicians. Bottomley gave him four priorities. Make quality central to NHS management, improve efficiency, handle strategic change in London and streamline the central management of the NHS. Langlands worked hard to reduce the number of national targets if for no other reason that "when you have more than 50

---

[166] NHS Funding and Expenditure. House of Commons Library.SN/SG/724.April 2012
[167] Led by Tim Chessells and Bob Nichols.
[168] The other two NHS candidates were Brian Edwards and Ken Jarrold.

priorities in truth you have none at all". Bottomley gave Langlands the freedom to create a clear identity for the NHS Management Executive. A Communications Director was duly appointed, and NHS Executive annual reports began to appear.

In 1995 the Calman/Hine[169] report started the process of reshaping cancer services. The Department of Health was entering deeper and deeper into clinical practice. The work on quality however was still focused on patient experience rather than clinical outcomes.

Bottomley was a Secretary of State who sought to calm things down and make the NHS work. She consolidated the work of others rather than launch new and radical ideas of her own. She claimed to believe in a greater degree of independence for the NHS but when she had the opportunity to think seriously about an independent corporation during the internal debates about "the intermediate tier" she dismissed it quite quickly on the grounds that it would only create yet another organisation to press the government for more funds.[170] She was however always positive about the importance of the NHS Executive which although based in Leeds had retained offices in Richmond House close to her office. Although like all politicians she could not resist straying into day to day operational matters when the media was involved, by and large she left managers to get on with the job and left some space for the NHS Executive to develop.

She curbed and softened [some might say smothered] the internal market and moved the NHS closer back to its public service roots. Like most of her predecessors she invested a lot of her time in NHS and Departmental restructuring which produced few benefits. In this regard she may have been unduly influenced by Brian Mawhinney her Minister of State.[171]

She worked her officials hard with constant telephone contact and drew into her circle leaders from within the NHS who often accompanied her when she gave evidence to House of Commons Select Committees.

---

[169] Calman and Hine were the CMO's of England and Wales.
[170] The Executive Years of the NHS. Edwards and Fall. 2005.
[171] He was replaced in 1994 by Gerry Malone.

She was rather liked by her civil service colleagues and the two Chief Executives of the NHS with whom she worked[172]. She had a very mixed public persona and a reputation for reeling off lots of statistics in interviews rather than presenting political ideas. One journalist described her response to questions as Teflon coated…they could mean anything. Despite her undoubted social values and commitment to the ideals of the NHS she was voted the most insincere politician in Britain in a Daily Telegraph poll. She never tried to get close to the media which may have been a mistake. A senior BMA man said that whilst he did not think she had been very good as a minister she would have made a brilliant ward sister. A backhanded compliment if ever there was one. She strongly encouraged Alan Langlands to build effective working relationships with the BMA and the other health professions and in this he had some success.

She was a better Secretary of State than the media gave her credit for being. It was, she said, the job that most marked her career in politics. She displayed no great visions of her own about the future of the NHS, but she had kept the service moving down the road set by Kenneth Clarke but at a slower and more cautious pace. Nobody, including her critics, doubted her values.

In July 1995 she moved on to become Secretary of State for National Heritage.

She resigned her seat at the 2005 general election and entered the Lords as Baroness Bottomley of Nettlestone. She took on a number of executive and non-executive posts in business including BUPA and the international head hunters Odgers. She strongly supported the Lansley reforms in the House of Lords. By this time, she was beginning to have doubts about how long the NHS could survive in its present form." It will get to 70 years but what happens after that?".

1948-Date

---

[172] Nichol and Langlands.

Stephen Dorrell

July 1995-May 1997

Conservative

Stephen Dorrell was born in Worcestershire and educated at Uppingham School and Brasenose College, Oxford. On leaving university he worked in his family industrial clothing business.

He entered the House of Commons in 1979 as MP for Loughborough in Leicestershire.[173] Aged 27 he was the youngest member of this Parliament. Margaret Thatcher appointed him to the Whip's office in 1987. In 1990 he was appointed Parliamentary Under Secretary of State at the Department of Health where he joined first Ken Clarke and then William Waldegrave.

After the 1992 general election he became Financial Secretary to the Treasury and then Secretary of State for Heritage when he joined the cabinet of John Major.

In 1995 he became Secretary of State for Health and remained in post until the general election in 1997. He came in with a good knowledge of health and a reputation as a competent minister with a mind of his own and a belief in sound economics. The Labour opposition regarded him as a" very able guy but he was sent in to play a dead bat". He later acknowledged this himself "If you take office in the last two years of an eighteen-year spell your chances of leaving great monuments are relatively remote."[174]

---

[173] In 1997 due to a boundary change he became MP for Charnwood in Leicestershire.
[174] Health Services Journal NHS at 60 Supplement.

He saw his job as giving the Clarke reforms the chance to breathe and draw out as much of the political venom as he could. He had been a junior minister in health when the Clarke reforms had been launched. He wanted to concentrate on solving practical problems rather than have furious ideological debates. He demanded a 5% cut in management costs which he judged could be justified now that the main reorganisation pressures were off. He was not by instinct a centraliser. "No big business in the world, no other human activity, even including the military, any longer believes that the efficient way of delivering a defined objective is to concentrate all power at the centre"[175] His White paper "A Service with Ambition" got wide support and was seen by some as the precursor to the Labour reforms that were to follow. The white paper committed the Conservatives to a publicly funded, high quality NHS available to all based on clinical need. A primary care led NHS was, it claimed, the way forward providing services to well informed citizens. A major IT investment was crucial to the future as was a more skilled workforce. The paper also argued the case for more integrated health care. He encouraged experiments with total purchasing pilots where GPs managed almost all their patient budgets.

He had to deal with some of the excesses of the internal market in Yorkshire following criticism by the National Audit Office. The Chief Executive was sacked by Alan Langlands on the grounds that he was not a fit person to be part of the new NHS. The NHS was a public sector internal market.

His Primary Care Act was passed with all party support. Health Authorities were to be given the responsibility for raising standards and improving access to primary care. The salaried GP [which the BMA had stoutly resisted for years] was to be a real option and nurse

---

[175] Edwards and Fall. Nuffield Trust.

prescribing was to be extended. There would be a determined effort to reduce the paperwork in general practice. Dorrell had effectively deregulated General Practice and opened the door to new models of contract and employment. All of this would demand increased investment, but little was available. The NHS was heading for negative growth and only secured 0.5% in 1996/7. Dorrell knew and acknowledged that as the NHS became more successful demand would rise.

The Health of the Nation policies rolled on and the Department led by Kenneth Calman the CMO was now searching more determinedly for ways of dealing with the striking differences in life expectancy, morbidity and mortality by social class, region and ethnic background.[176] The 4th anniversary of the launch of the Health of the Nation policy was marked by a grand national conference in July 1996. Progress was noted across the board. Dorrell pushed strongly for improved partnerships in mental health with a green paper in February 1997. At around this time the first reports began to emerge of vCJD [Mad Cow disease] which led to new food safety regulations.

His relationships with the health professions was reasonably good. He explained" There is also a balance to be achieved with clinicians who want to feel their judgement is respected. They want the freedom to do what they see as being in the best interests of their patients-and that is right and proper and good but has to be balanced against value for money and efficiency.[177]

In September 1995 he approved a deal with the TUC which allowed local pay bargaining within a national framework. The push to devolve pay bargaining was to continue with little success.

---

[176] On the State of the Public Health.1995.
[177] Dorrell. The greatest experiment. The NHS at 60.

He rejigged the NHS Policy Board when first appointed with a focus entirely on the management of the NHS but eventually closed it down. It added little value he explained.

The Child B case in Cambridgeshire had opened up the issue of rationing in the NHS and some Health Authorities started to specify which treatments were not to be provided by the NHS [tattoo removals and the like]. But Dorrell was against this approach and would not allow any blanket bans on treatment." There will always be the exceptional case where treatment can be clinically justified". Ministers saw the dangers of having to accept the responsibility for decisions about individual patients...that was a matter for clinicians. Purchasing was becoming a problem and needed to become more sophisticated and sensitive." Nobody expects health managers to spend money on moonshine, equally they must leave room for uncertainty and risk taking" said Dorrell. Post code rationing, as it was labelled by Labour, was also emerging as a problem but Dorrell resisted the argument that central government should decide what treatments should be available on the NHS. Some years later GP commissioners produced long lists of excluded treatments demonstrating that clinicians could ration more effectively than politicians.

Alan Langlands the Chief Executive was also backpedalling furiously against those managers and GPs who were adopting hard line purchasing policies. He put it more vividly "I do distance myself not just emotionally but logically from the ration and privatise brigade "The internal market had its boundaries and limits and a Labour government was just around the corner.

As the general election approached the NHS came under renewed pressure as the system tried to cope with low growth, reducing waiting lists and dealing with an increasing number of medical emergencies.[178]

Dorrell got on well with Graham Hart his Permanent Secretary and with Alan Langlands the NHS Chief Executive who described him as a non-interventionist Chairman, a big picture Chairman, who was interested in ideas and did not get bogged down in detail. Dorrell had also got on well when he was a junior health minister with Duncan Nichol the former NHS Chief Executive.

After the general election, when Frank Dobson took over, Dorrell kept the shadow health brief for a time. In 2010 he was elected Chair of the Health Select Committee. He remains of the view that the core idea of the NHS is still sound, but the model needs to change so that "it loses its image of being a state charity for which we should all be grateful".

He stood down as an MP in 2015 and took up the Chair of the NHS Confederation He joined the Board of several private companies. He also chaired the Birmingham and Solihull Transformation Board which was trying to find a way forward for the NHS in one of the most culturally diverse parts of the country.

He left his successor Frank Dobson a portrait of Cromwell in the Whitehall office. It was, Dobson said, the only thing he would keep as he promised to wind up the internal market in the NHS.

---

[178] Medical admissions were up 37% on the previous year,

FRANK DOBSON

May 1997-October 1999

Labour

Frank Dobson was born in York the son of a railwayman. He graduated from LSE with an economics degree in 1962.His early career was in the Electricity industry. He became heavily involved in London politics and became leader of Camden Council in 1973.He stood down as leader in 1975 to become Assistant Secretary at the office of the Local Government Ombudsman. He entered Parliament as Labour MP for Holborn and St Pancras in 1979 and by 1987 began to shadow a series of Conservative ministers [Leader of the House, Energy, Employment, Transport and Environment].

He proved to be an engaging and convivial politician with a pugnacious style. When Tony Blair appointed him Secretary of State for Health in 1997, he chose as his political advisor Simon Stevens who was later to become the Chief Executive of NHS England. His Minister of State was Alan Milburn and later John Denham. He had two powerful women as junior ministers; Jowell and Jay. Gisela Stuart was an extra minister. Blair want her to become the Minister for NHS Direct, but Dobson thought this inappropriate. Lord Hunt was to join his team in 1998.

Health had been a major issue during the election with Labour claiming that the British public had "24 hours to save the NHS".

On appointment he immediately announced the abolition of the internal market in the NHS which led eventually to a White Paper, [The New NHS: Modern, Dependable[179]] which launched Primary Care Groups to replace GP Fund Holding. The NHS was now to focus on integrated care based on partnership and driven by performance and transparency. He declared his intention to start a ten-year programme to renew and improve the NHS through evolutionary change rather than organisational upheaval. The new NHS would, he claimed, have quality at its heart and the experience of users

---

[179] Cmnd 3807.December 1997.

would shape policy. There would be a national survey of patient and user experience.

The weakness of the NHS, he later explained, was its vulnerability to the problem of short political timescales; Ministers making changes and wanting instant gratification.[180]

Seven months later came a consultative paper entitled "A First-Class Service" which laid out plans for reducing the huge variation in clinical practice in the NHS in areas such as conservation surgery for breast cancer and knee replacements. He wanted clear national standards but with the responsibility for delivery lying with local health organisations. He created NICE which would provide the framework for standard setting as well as undertaking an agreed programme of systemic reviews. The first piece of guidance they issued was a rapid assessment of the influenza drug Zanamivir. This was followed by a series of national service frameworks for a number of clinical services [elderly, mental health, cancer and diabetes]. The government was deep into clinical territory. NICE would become a world leader in health technology assessment.[181] The Commission for Health Improvement would monitor progress. An information strategy emerged in September 1988 alongside a human resource strategy. Pay would be settled nationally but with room for local variation.

Clinical governance was introduced which demanded clear lines of accountability for clinical quality, procedures for managing risk and the identification of poor clinical performance. Clinical indicators were added to NHS performance league tables. The number of places at England's medical schools was increased by 1000. [182]Dobson had no great fights with the BMA and the health professions. They understood his commitment to the NHS and how hard he was prepared to fight for its future. He was not an instinctive moderniser.

Nurses rather liked him. In 1999 he had published Making a Difference which had forecast the development of nurse consultants, nurse prescribing and

---

[180] Rejuvenate or retire. Views of the NHS at 60. Nuffield Trust.
[181] National Institute for Clinical Excellence. Later renamed National Institute for Health and Care Excellence. It became a Non-Departmental Public Body in 2013.
[182] New medical schools appeared in Norwich [2000], Peninsula [2000], Warwick [2000], Durham [2001], Brighton [2002], Lancaster [2004]and Hull [2004].

personal development plans for nurses. It included a new model of nurse education. Alan Milburn was later to accelerate progress in these areas in his NHS Plan.

Dobson demanded a purge of "Tory deadbeats" on NHS Boards. He proceeded to appoint many labour activists to health organisations to such a degree that it provoked criticism from the Commissioner for Public Appointments. He brought in Greg Dyke to update the Patients Charter.[183]

He asked for yet another review of the NHS in London [Turnberg and English] which allowed him to "save St. Bart's for the nation". He persuaded Magdi Yacoub to move from Harefield Hospital to a new heart unit at St Mary's thus removing one of the principal blocks in the plan to concentrate some important London specialties in fewer units. He eventually opted for the creation of a single regional office for London.

He had strong views about bed reductions in the NHS and asked Clive Smee the senior health economist at the Department of Health to undertake a review of future bed needs. Bed numbers had been falling steadily from 1948 when 480,000 were available to 190,000 in 1998. The decline had been most acute in mental health with the switch to community care, but acute beds had also fallen sharply as lengths of stay reduced. Smee recommended more intermediate care beds to take the pressure off acute services.[184]

He encouraged Donald Acheson the CMO to publish his Inquiry into Inequalities in Health which recommended that all government policies be assessed for their impact on health inequality; that priority be given to women of child bearing age and children and that steps be taken to reduce income inequality. Once again, twenty years after the Black Report, the link between poverty and poor health came under the political spotlight. A mental health strategy was launched in December 1988. Community care for the mentally ill had failed, said Dobson, and must be strengthened.

Social care, another part of Dobson's huge empire was developing slowly with increased investment, much of it invested in independent sector providers. The Chief Inspector of Social Care reported great progress in moving vulnerable

---

[183] Dyke reported in December 1998.
[184] The Beds Inquiry reported in 2000 when Alan Milburn was Secretary of State

people out of vast isolated institutions into community care.[185] The big question as to who should pay for social care was given to a Royal Commission.

He had as a member of his ministerial team a Minister for Public Health [Tessa Jowell]. Together with Ken Calman the CMO they launched first a Green paper and then a White paper under the banner "Our Healthier Nation"[186],[187]. Four national priority areas for action by government and not just the Department of Health were identified. The priority areas were heart disease and stroke, accidents, cancer and mental health. Each had their own target to reach within a defined time frame. Targets were at the centre of much government policy under the Blair government. Health Action Zones were created to target health inequalities and plans were laid for a network of healthy living centres. A new Cabinet sub-committee was established to track progress.

Dobson authorised combined health and social care budgets. He set up the Inquiry into children's heart surgery at Bristol Royal Infirmary. He intervened to limit the prescription of Viagra. He authorised the PFI deal to build a new hospital in Norwich. He expanded the role of NHS Direct a telephone help line for patients.

Dobson led a busy ministerial team prodded on by the Prime Minister who wanted change and improvement in the NHS. The great difficulty was that whilst his claims to be unpicking the conservative internal market were popular, nobody was clear where the NHS was expected to be in five years' time.[188]

Towards the end of Dobson's term in office finance became a major issue again. He had secured just over 4% for 1998/9 but Health Authority deficits were accumulating at an alarming rate. In allocating the 1998/99 budget he earmarked £500 million for priority areas and waiting list reduction. Negotiations with the Treasury were now held twice a year and were renamed spending reviews.

---

[185] Better Management: Better Care. Chief Inspector Social Services Inspectorate. Annual Report 1996/97.
[186] Our Healthier Nation. Cmnd 3852.1998.
[187] Saving Lives. Our Healthier Nation. CM 4386. 1999.
[188] Peter Mandelson. The Third Man. Harper Press 2011

He secured £250m for winter pressures in November 1998 but it was not enough. Dobson told Blair that in the following year the NHS would need an extra £2 billion pounds if a crisis was to be avoided.

Dobson had little respect for the NHS Executive which he regarded as "second rate and incompetent" although he did eventually come to respect the skills of Alan Langlands the Chief Executive whose contract he extended. In October 1997 he recruited Phillip Hunt to join his ministerial team as spokesman in the Lords. He was scathing about the appointment of "dumbos" as Chief Executives in the NHS and sought to get involved in key appointments. He would have preferred the French system which would have enabled him to move the best managers into the major problem areas.[189] In future Chief Executives were to have a statutory responsibility for quality. Although he claimed to keep his distance in practice, he had no inhibitions at all about intervening in the day to day management of the NHS when he judged it to be politically necessary. He tried to run the NHS by command and control.

In January 1999 he received a report from an inquiry into events at Ashworth Special Hospital in Liverpool. He was angry about what had happened but declined to accept the recommendation that the hospital should close. He did however approve a major investment in enhanced security at all the special hospitals.

In March 1999 the Royal Commission on Long Term Care was published which called for free personal care to be made available from general taxation. He sat on it. It took Alan Milburn and the government a year and a half to respond and then little happened. The report was regarded by many politicians as hopelessly idealistic.

The civil service, as distinct from the NHS Executive, worked well with Dobson and his team but he did question whether the system needed both a Permanent Secretary and an NHS Chief Executive. The decision was left to his successor. Liam Donaldson took over as CMO in October 1998 with his experience both as a clinician and an NHS manager.

---

[189] The Executive Years of the NHS. Edwards and Fall. 2005.

Dobson resigned in October 1999 to stand as a candidate for the post of Mayor of London. He lost out to Ken Livingstone. Some who worked with him at the time thought Blair had "let him go "to install moderniser Milburn in place. He returned to the Commons in 2005 but not to ministerial office.

Dobson is an instinctive and engaging politician rather than a great thinker. He had a good, energetic team of ministers whilst at Health and chose a knowledgeable political advisor Simon Stevens who would later become Chief Executive of NHS England. He played his part in softening up Tony Blair for the major new investment that was to come during Alan Milburn's term of office. He and his team achieved a lot in a short time. Had he stayed in post he might have emerged as one of the very good ministers of health. It was to be his only ministerial post.

1940-Date

ALAN MILBURN

October 1999- June 2003

Labour

Alan Milburn was born on Tyneside. He read history at Lancaster University. He returned to Newcastle and got involved in many radical causes including battles to save jobs in the steel and shipbuilding industries. He was a CND activist.

He entered Parliament in 1992 as MP for Darlington. He was a strong supporter of Tony Blair in his attempts to modernise the Labour Party. When Labour came into power in 1997, he was appointed Minister of State at the Department of Health under Frank Dobson. He drove through the PFI programme for hospital development. Like his boss, Milburn was not impressed with NHS management "We had to inject some steel into the spine of the NHS and ramrod change from the centre "he said. He was only in post for a little over eighteen months when he was promoted to the Cabinet as Chief Secretary to the Treasury.

He returned to Health as Secretary of State in October 1999. He came into office and announced that he intended to proceed with the radical reform of the NHS. The NHS cannot afford to stay still, he argued. He would, he said, take on any vested interests that tried to block modernisation. The doctors were, he said, in the last chance saloon. "If the NHS did not change it would die". He created his own strategy unit inside the Department of Health[190] to prepare an NHS Plan and effectively side lined the NHS Executive led by Alan Langlands. Langlands resigned in February 2000 to take up the post of Vice Chancellor at Dundee University. He left with plaudits from Milburn about excellent service to the NHS, but the role of chief executive had been seriously diminished by Milburn.[191] Milburn asked Neil McKay the deputy Chief Executive to cover the job whilst he thought about the future. He wanted to get on with developing a new plan with all the new money that he had been promised by Tony Blair.

The millennium bug never materialised to test NHS preparedness.

In June 2000 Milburn returned to an idea first canvassed by Dobson and decided to combine the posts of Chief Executive of the NHS and Permanent Secretary. The post was advertised. The surprise appointment was Nigel Crisp, an NHS manager with almost no profile outside Oxford and London. He was quiet and unassuming but with a reputation as a strategic thinker. Milburn expected to provide the spark and drive himself. With his new Modernisation Board operating Milburn decided that the NHS Executive could be wound up. It was a nonsense he said, and its independence was a fiction.[192] Crisp agreed with him. Nigel Crisp created his own Management Board in London. The NHS Executive and its regional offices were formally wound up in 2002 and 28 Strategic Health Authorities were appointed who supervised the performance of Primary Care Trusts. It was another major reorganisation that would cost a fortune, achieve little and slow down the momentum of change.

The Beds Inquiry which had concluded that the health system did not have the right beds in the right place reported in 2000 and was fed into the work on the

---

[190] Led by Chris Hamm who would later become Chief Executive at the Kings Fund in London.
[191] Langlands had had his contract extended in 1999. He got on well with Tony Blair.
[192] The Executive Years of the NHS. Edwards and Fall.

NHS Plan as was a report by the CMO, Liam Donaldson *An Organisation with a Memory* which promoted quality by improving safety. In his foreword to this report Milburn acknowledged the complexity of modern health care and the challenge this presented in making the NHS as safe a place as possible for patients. A new National Patient Safety Authority was created in 2001 which operated a national system for reporting and analysing adverse health events.[193] Meanwhile ten multidisciplinary task forces started work on the NHS Plan but at this point they still had no clear idea about its financial foundations. Nevertheless, the health professions were pleased to be heavily involved in planning the future.

Lord Winston, the infertility specialist and Labour peer, caused a storm in January 2000 with serious complaints about the NHS treatment of his mother. The Labour government had he said been deceitful in its promise to properly fund the NHS. The BMA and the Medical Royal Colleges waded in behind him. On Sunday 16th January 2000 Blair stunned everybody by announcing that within five years NHS funding would match the European average.... a rise of 25%.[194] Gordon Brown delivered the first tranche of new money in his March 2000 budget and promised a growth rate of over 5% in each of the following three years. It was to be the biggest expenditure boost in the history of the NHS with a five-year moving average over the period 1999/2000 to 2003/4 of 7.6%.

Gordon Brown who had been pushed into this investment by Blair [but was later to embrace it] launched his own Treasury review of NHS funding led by Derek Wanless a former banker. He had concluded in an interim report in November 2001, designed to coincide with Brown's budget statement, that there was no evidence that an alternative funding system would deliver a given quality of health care at a lower cost to the tax payer. Wanless produced a series of scenarios about future spending which pretty much matched the projections made by the Department of Health. The NHS needed 7.3% real time growth for five years followed by steady investment that would lead to the NHS taking up 12.5% of GDP by 2022/23. He was critical of NHS productivity which explained to some degree the Treasury pressure in the

---

[193] The organisation was closed down in 2012 and its functions transferred to NHS England.
[194] In 1999 the UK spent 6.9% GDP compared with France 10.1% and Germany 10.3%.

coming years to increase efficiency targets. The first investment step was to be taken but the follow up got lost in the economic crisis that was building.

The NHS Plan when it emerged in July 2000 had the formal support of the health professions and trade unions all of whom had been involved in the working parties that formed the base for the plan. The final version had been written by Milburn himself. Thousands of new consultants,[195] general practitioners, nurses and therapists were to be recruited and the number of training places expanded. Modern matrons would oversee progress on the ground. Waiting lists would tumble with the help of diagnostic and treatment centres operated by the private sector.[196] There would be national standards for major conditions and standard protocols. Routine screening would be extended. New intermediate care services would take the pressure off acute beds and 100 new hospitals would be built. PFI would be expanded into primary care with LIFT programmes. Walk in centres would provide citizens with immediate access to skilled care. NHS Direct would be expanded. Millions of pounds were earmarked for improved cleaning and catering in hospitals.

The Plan was not just about the NHS. It covered social care which had its own targets and authorised the creation of single organisations to commission both health and social care. The first Health and Social Care Trusts began to form from 2002. The government had buried the Royal Commission recommendation for free personal care but did agree to provide free nursing care in care homes.

With the new plan came a new bureaucracy including a Modernisation Board chaired by Alan Milburn and a Modernisation Agency to identify and spread best practice.[197] The membership of the Modernisation Board included many of the key figures from the NHS. It never had an executive role, but Milburn listened to the advice and opinions offered by its members. This was another attempt to lock in the professions and for a time it worked. It faded away when Milburn moved on.

---

[195] 1000 new medical school places and two new medical schools.
[196] The first contracts were let in September 2003.
[197] The Agency would incorporate a new NHS Leadership Centre

Sensitive to the criticism by Len Peach the Appointments Commissioner he decided that Non-Executive Directors of NHS boards would in future be appointed not by ministers but by an independent Appointments Commission. Patronage which had often been behind paid NHS appointments was removed.

The NHS plan was not a vision for radical change in the NHS but for the modernisation of the existing system. In the Wanless scenarios it was "catch up money". It came with many targets and "must do's "to ensure that all the new money was spent as planned along with an ill-fated star system so that the public could judge performance and providers could secure earned autonomy. Community Health Councils were to be abolished.

The NHS Plan was widely and warmly welcomed and in the short term took a lot of pressure out of the system and healed the fractured relationships between government and the health professions. It was launched as a ten-year programme of rebuilding and renewing the NHS. There are those who now think of the NHS Plan as just a huge sticking plaster covering up historic funding problems rather than a strategic plan to secure the long-term future of the NHS. Those of this view regard the massive investment as having been largely wasted and of laying the seeds of the financial crisis to come. The first tranche was indeed soaked up in meeting existing debt and national targets. There was little left for locally inspired growth. This tension between national targets and local discretion was a constant issue during Milburn's term in office.[198]

The one exception to the celebratory mood was Community Health Councils who were shocked at their planned demise. They fought hard to stay but eventually disappeared in December 2003.

Now the plan was set the Department of Health would, it was promised, resume steering rather than rowing the NHS. The NHS could no longer be run from the centre the politicians had concluded. Millburn may have been influenced to some degree by the hard time he was given when bodies were found stored in an unrefrigerated chapel at Bedford Hospital. It was very much a local problem, but the media wanted him to be accountable.

---

[198] Nigel Crisp.24 Hours to save the NHS.OUP.2011

He appointed Lord Laming to conduct an inquiry into the death of Victoria Climbie.[199]

He and his team planned a radical overhaul of the bodies that inspected for quality in health and social care. The Health Care Commission chaired by Ian Kennedy, who had led the Bristol Inquiry, took over the role from three other bodies in 2004[200]. A National Clinical Assessment Authority was created to help NHS Boards deal with difficult doctors. Crisp reported that the quality structures in the NHS were as good as anywhere else in the world. The Stafford Inquiry would later demonstrate that this was simply not true.

In 2002 the Tobacco Advertising and Promotion Act came into operation.

The push to reduce waiting times for non-emergency surgery continued with some considerable success. This was what patients had put close to the top of their wish lists in their focus groups.

Milburn was now taking the NHS well beyond the Thatcher reforms. He was contemplating franchising out parts of NHS management. He no longer wanted to run a nationalised industry but oversee a system of care.

The satisfaction within the NHS generated by the NHS Plan did not last long. The medical profession was being hit from all sides by the media. The GMC, who had a particularly hard time, had a story every week about medical scandals and poor clinical practice. Dr Harold Shipman was just one of the most prominent.[201] Milburn moved to try to prevent what the Times called a meltdown in the relationship between the doctors and the government, but events were now moving against him. Money earmarked at the centre for services like cancer never seemed to arrive at the coal face. Family doctors were threatening unofficial action and Peter Hawker Chairman of the BMA Consultants Committee claimed that the NHS would collapse unless the government stopped pushing up patient expectations. Yet another fight about the Consultants contract was to rumble on until 2003.

---

[199] It reported in January 2003

[200] It only lasted five years until CQC took over in 2009.

[201] Dr Shipman murdered many of his patients. He was arrested in 1998 and came to trial in 2000. The Inquiry that followed reported in January 2005.

In June 2003 just as Milburn was about to leave office a deal was struck with the BMA about general practice. GPs got a substantial pay rise if they met a series of quality targets[202] and were allowed to opt out of a twenty-four-hour commitment to their practice patients.[203] Health authorities now had to organise GP out of hours emergency care. The majority of GPs elected to opt out and lost only 6% of their contract income. Given the 30% rise in income this was a small price to pay.

Milburn was now a full convert to localism. The government had to do less, and the NHS had to do more. Inside the Department the top team created by Nigel Crisp looked very much like a replacement for the NHS Executive except that in the search for inclusiveness his top team meetings often had 50 people present. The target culture still dominated the life of managers whose jobs were at risk if important targets were missed. Some managers began to fiddle the waiting list figures and had to be sacked. Many gave overly optimistic statements about the state of their finances. Events like the winter crisis in 2001/2 demanded strong national action. Ian Bogle the chair of the BMA accused the government of providing care based on numbers and corporate bullying. Milburn's mind may have turned to localism but in the real world the centre still dominated.

This centralist message was reinforced in 2002 when a national agreement was struck with trade unions about NHS pay. "Achieving a Balance" swept away a myriad of deals struck in various Whitley Councils and replaced them with a single pay spine. NHS Employers [part of the NHS Confederation] took over from the Whitley system. NHS Trusts could strike their own local deals but most elected to remain within the national system.

In 2002 the government upped the pace of change in response to the Wanless report but only after furious rows between Blair, Brown, Milburn and Balls. Successful hospitals would be further liberated from Whitehall on becoming Foundation Hospitals. They would be accountable to their local governors and not the Secretary of State. It was planned that all NHS hospitals would eventually operate as Foundation Trusts. Their freedoms were real but not completely unfettered. Gordon Brown as Chancellor of the Exchequer insisted

---

[202] Quality and Outcomes framework,
[203] The Blue Book.

on limiting their borrowing powers. The private sector would be encouraged to support the NHS and patients were to be offered budgets like the direct payments in social care. This was not what the leaders of the health professions had signed up for. The enthusiasm that had been generated by the Hospital Plan only two years earlier had been dissipated.[204] Crisp talked about overstretch and a loss of momentum.

Lord Hunt one of his ministerial team resigned on a point of principle in 2003 following the invasion of Iraq.

Milburn resigned in June 2003 to spend more time with his family, but he was according to Peter Mandelson [205] almost certainly worn out and fed up with his constant battles with Gordon Brown. He was succeeded by John Reid.

Alan Milburn was a politician who learned whilst he was in office and moved from being a centralist to a localist. He drew the BMA, Trade Unions and staff of the NHS into his work on the NHS Plan, but he got little long-term credit for doing so. It was he who led the target culture and for this he was unrepentant. He closed the NHS Executive. He had no inhibitions about encouraging partnerships between the NHS and the private sector which for a Labour politician must register as a brave move.

He later described his journey as a transition between "one system which is a mid-twentieth century way of organising care that is top down, monopoly provided and driven by the interests of the producers rather than consumers towards a system which is more bottom up, is more diversified in terms of its provider base and which is ruled by the interests of patients". The challenge he claimed was to retain the collectivist model but attune it to a more individualised world.[206]

His term of office was full of early promise particularly as the Blair dividend began to appear. The problem was the lack of a clearly expressed vision of the medium-term future. It always felt like the NHS Plan was about refurbishing yesterday's NHS rather than building a new NHS with a long-term future. It could be that the long-term future, which he later explained would be firmly

---

[204] 24Hours to save the NHS. Nigel Crisp.
[205] Peter Mandelson. The Third Man. Harper Press 2011
[206] Rejuvenate or Retire. Nuffield Trust.

based on the interests of patients, would only emerged slowly. Or he might have recognised the challenge his ideas would present to the vested interests in the NHS and to some within his own party, that he thought twice about spelling them out.

He thought and acted as if he was the Chief Executive of the NHS at least in his early years in office. He did not get on well with Chris Kelly his permanent secretary.

He stood down as an MP in 2010 and moved on to chair the Commission on Social Mobility and Child Poverty between 2012 and 2017.

He returned to front line politics quite quickly and has clearly influenced the Labour Party in its thinking about the NHS and its future which in his view lies with local government commissioning NHS care from independent NHS Trusts.

1958-date.

JOHN REID

June 2003- May 2005

Labour

John Reid was born in Cardowan a mining village near Motherwell. He left school at 16 and worked in the construction and insurance industry. He joined the Communist Party in 1972 and later switched to Labour. He studied at Stirling University from 1971 gaining a BA in history and a PhD in economic history. His doctorate was on the 19th Century West African slave trade. During 1979-1983 he was the research officer for the Labour Party in Scotland. He then moved on to become an advisor to Neil Kinnock and the Scottish organiser of Trade Unionists for Labour. He entered Parliament at the 1987 general election as MP for Motherwell North. Until the early 1980s he was a close ally of Gordon Brown, but the relationship broke down. By this time, he had a growing problem with alcohol which was only solved when John Smith the Labour Leader gave him an ultimatum to stop drinking or leave politics which he heeded. His first ministerial appointment was at Defence which he loved. He later became Secretary of State for Northern Ireland it must be said with mixed success. His appointment to Health following Alan Milburn was no great surprise; it was his fourth Cabinet post in a year. John Hutton who had been a health minister since 1998 stayed on as Reid's deputy. Reid's first task was to calm down the doctors. He agreed handsome pay rises for both GP's and Consultants and perhaps most controversially allowed GP's to opt out of night and weekend work.[207] Both settlements cost far more than had been estimated and fuelled the financial crisis for his successors.

With his NHS Improvement Plan published towards the end of 2003 he fixed the eighteen-week target from referral by a GP to treatment and brought in private sector treatment centres to assist the NHS in reducing waiting times. He opened the NHS market to any provider who could meet the NHS quality standards and charge at or under the NHS Tariff. The choice policy was not universally popular, and many NHS consultants and managers hated the idea that their referral base might be weakened as patients chose other NHS or private sector providers.

He responded to the Laming report on child protection by announcing the biggest reorganisation of children's services in 30 years. A green paper "Every Child Matters" led to the Children's Act 2004.

He was a strong supporter of volunteers in the NHS.

The first tranche of Foundation hospitals came on stream in April 2004. The approval process had proved to be much more challenging than anticipated as the finances of many potential Foundation trusts were beginning to deteriorate.

He told the NHS in no uncertain terms to bring down hospital acquired infection rates. He insisted that NHS matrons be put in charge of cleaning staff. Infection rates began to slowly reduce. He wanted a ban on smoking in all places that served food and was to fight a furious battle with his successor Patricia Hewitt when she extended it to a complete ban.

In late 2004 a white paper "choosing health" signalled the governments approach to supporting people to make health choices in a consumer society. It also highlighted the challenge of obesity.

In health he reinforced his reputation as the New Labour bruiser and fixer. He was only in post for two years before he moved on again to the job he most wanted which was Secretary of State for Defence.

On the civil service network Reid was admired for mastering his brief and making decisions. Some commentators observed a pattern of behaviour of always siding with his civil servants which is perhaps not surprising given the speed with which he moved through Whitehall departments. He was not overly political in his time at Health. He told a Labour conference that their health policy should focus on increasing patient power.

His relationship with the NHS Confederation was never good. They blamed him for a breach of faith between the Department of Health and the NHS. He was not a man for extensive consultation. Jeremy Paxton called him an all-purpose attack dog less concerned with promoting Labour policy than trying to put the opposition into intensive care.

He was never an inspirational Minister of Health.

He moved to the Ministry of Defence in 2005 and then to the Home Office in 2006.

He retired from government in 2007 when Tony Blair resigned and did not contest his seat in 2010.

He joined the House of Lords as Lord Reid of Cardowan.

1947-date

PATRICIA HEWITT

May 2005-June 2007

Labour

Patricia Hewitt was born in Australia. Her father was a senior civil servant. After nine years as, General Secretary of the National Council for Civil Liberties she became press secretary to Neil Kinnock. She played a key role in the modernisation of the Labour Party. She had a reputation as a high profile left winger and for almost five years worked as deputy director of the left leaning Institute for Public Policy Research. Between 1994-1997 she was head of research at Anderson Consulting. In 1997 she became MP for Leicester East a safe Labour seat.

In 2001 she joined Tony Blair's Cabinet as Secretary of State for Trade and Industry and Minister for Women and Equality. She moved to Health in May 2005.

The 2005 Labour Election Manifesto had signalled the way forward. Now that the NHS had been "revived" a system would be built with the patient in the driving seat, free to all and personal to each citizen. The Manifesto effectively buried the Labour party opposition to competition in the health sector.[208]

On the face of it she had a series of strong ministerial teams with Rosie Winterton, Norman Warner, Jane Kennedy, Caroline Flint, Andy Burnham and Phillip Hunt who had returned to government office.

Almost the first thoughts of the new team were another reorganisation or *streamlining* as they liked to call it. The Department of Health was to be cut by a third and £500 million was to be saved by reorganising the NHS.

The number of PCT's was to be sharply reduced as was the number of Strategic Health Authorities. Nigel Crisp, the NHS Chief Executive and his team argued for a radical but slower pace of change than ministers had in mind. The final decision was communicated to the NHS in July 2005. Practice based

---

[208] Norman Warner. A suitable case for treatment.GHP.2011.

commissioning was to be in place right across the country by the end of 2006. The number of SHAs would be reduced to 10 and 302 PCTs reduced to 152, Ambulance trusts would be reduced from 32 to 11. Almost 190 NHS organisations had been culled.[209] It was as one minister put it a messy and brutal process.[210] Ministers did look briefly at options for an Independent NHS [as did Gus O'Donnell the Cabinet Secretary] but nothing came of it until Andrew Lansley created NHS England in 2012.[211]

The second half of 2005 was the UK turn at the Presidency of the EU with major conferences on health inequalities and patient safety.

The Foundation Trust movement was growing steadily and had been actively encouraged. Primary Care Trusts were told to press on with GP commissioning, but few did. Few PCTs believed it was possible.

In December 2005 Nigel Crisp the Chief Executive of the NHS and Permanent Secretary presented a very upbeat report. Waiting times for non-emergency care were down sharply and patient satisfaction was high. The growth in the early years of Milburn's NHS Plan had been enormous. Between September 1999 and September 2004 there had been 68,000 extra nurses, 26,000 professional and technical staff, 7500 Consultants and an additional 3330 General Practitioners. 30% of the new money had gone in pay rises for staff. The average growth rate between 2005/6 and 2007/8 was expected to be 7.1% but then the bonanza would be over. There was no mention in Crisp's report of the impending financial crisis nor according to Norman Warner, the Minister of State, had there been any warnings in ministerial briefings when they took up office. The NHS was overheating badly as all the new staff increased activity and with it cost.

Much of ministers' early energy was spent wrestling with the mechanics of the internal market. In December 2005 the NHS Choices web site started to operate and began to offer patients between four and five providers for their NHS care. This was not a universally popular move as Trusts began to fret about a loss of business sometimes to their own Consultant medical staff operating in private practice. The new standard Tariff [PBR] would reward

---

[209] One member of the ministerial team wanted to go further and cull 80 more.
[210] A Suitable case for treatment. Norman Warner.
[211] An Independent NHS. Edwards. Nuffield Trust. 2005.

Trusts for activity and provide a common playing field for the non-NHS sector to compete on. However, its impact on the more complex specialties was uncertain. The new tariff was applied to the acute sector in 2006/7. Despite the efforts of ministers, the private and independent sector found it hard to break into core NHS territory.

The growing financial problem began to emerge more clearly in the Spring of 2006. The accumulated debts in the system were growing and it became clear that some had not been fully declared to the Department of Health. Some Regions enforced, a much resented, pooling of reserves within regions which made a modest contribution to the problem but there was no room left in central budgets to cover deficits on the scale predicted. The Treasury had made a raid on central budgets [£800m] which largely removed the ability to offset overspends in one part of the NHS against others. The NHS was heading for a major overspend which was projected to be £1 billion. [212]

After years of amazingly high growth Hewitt found herself in the middle of a major NHS austerity programme. She took a very tough line with those NHS organisations in financial difficulties. There would be no hiding place for poor performers. It was unfair, she said, that those Trusts that had managed their affairs within budget should be expected to hand over their hard-won reserves to those Trusts who were overspending. Previously agreed loans were called in or had their timescales reduced. Turnaround teams descended on those Trusts in serious in difficulty. Hewitt threatened to resign if she could not drag the NHS out of a financial deficit and made it plain to NHS managers that securing breakeven was now the top priority. Inside the Department ministers had effectively taken over from Nigel Crisp and his team as they poured over spreadsheets, action plans and recovery projections.

Nigel Crisp fell on his sword in March 2006 as the debts accumulated and he lost the confidence of both ministers and senior people in the NHS. The final straw according to one minister was a fiery meeting of the Parliamentary Labour Party who reacted badly to his public comment that PCT's would be forced to divest themselves of some services they were currently running. He should have seen the crisis coming and intervened earlier even if that would

---

[212] In practice the NHS ran itself into a more modest deficit of £500m in 2005/6.

have put him at odds with his ministers. He was the Accounting Officer. He retired with a seat in the Lords. His quiet inclusive style was more suited to growth than the harsh world of retrenchment. In September 2006 David Nicholson took over as Chief Executive of the NHS and started to demand financial discipline. The combination of the Chief Executive post and that of the Permanent Secretary had ended. Hugh Taylor moved into the Permanent Secretary post.

Against the odds the NHS was hauled back into balance and in 2006/7 the NHS ended up with an overall surplus but 30,000 less staff. Ministers refused to write off historic debt and insisted that future brokerage should carry interest. For some of the larger trusts the agony was to continue. During 2006/7 £800 million in loans were issued to 50 NHS Trusts with payment, including interest spread over between 1 and 25 years.

The NHS was becoming increasingly dependent on computing systems to run the market and its associated quality systems. A national strategy had been published in 1998 but was running into trouble. It had grown like topsy and had seen a number of important contractor changes. Connecting for Health took over the management of the programme in April 2005. In the spring of 2006 one of the major contractors ran into trouble. David Nicholson moved to make SHAs responsible for implementation.[213] If the NHS did not believe in the plan it would not work, he explained.

Infection rates in England's hospitals were reaching alarming levels in 2006/7 and led amongst many other things to the launch of a national hand washing campaign in January 2007. The public began to ask questions about safety as they prepared for non-emergency surgery.

Meanwhile ministers had been thinking about the future. Their vision was compressed in a White Paper in 2006 *"Our health, Our care, Our say"*. The policy was produced after an extensive public consultation exercise including a huge citizen's panel meeting in Birmingham at which ministers were present. The result of this exercise was unsurprising. The public believed in prevention

---

[213] The National Audit office was later to report that in 2006/7 over 14,000 front line systems had been installed and the NHS was still in line to make major savings.

and wanted personalised service with rapid access. Top of their wish list were health checks, mental wellbeing, more help for carers and a trained nurse as first point of contact for patients. Many wanted the right to hold their personal health record on a smart card.

Hewitt and her team decided that patients would have more choice, care would become more personalised and citizens would be empowered to look after their own health. There would be new life check services and more talking therapies. The quality programmes in general practice would be tweaked to give greater emphasis to wellbeing outcomes. Bowel cancer screening would be extended, and clinical work would move in the direction of primary care. A new breed of community hospitals would be built. The closure of small hospitals was banned.[214]

A second White Paper set out the action plan. Ministers were enthusiastic, but the NHS was deep in the middle of a major retrenchment exercise. A few pilot schemes were launched but the system was focused on controlling expenditure in the acute sector. Hewitt had told managers to sort out the financial mess and this is what they did. Grand new strategy visions would have to wait. Many of the ideas in the White Paper emerged in the later Darzi reports during Alan Johnson's term of office.

Patient Forums, the replacement for Community Health Councils, would it was thought provide a stronger patient voice. In practice they were a disaster. Direct payments to citizens were to be accelerated in social care and thinking began about the practicalities of extending this policy into health.

Hewitt had a hard time at NHS Trade Union conferences where she was booed and heckled. In 2006 she endured 50 minutes of cat calls, barracking and derisive laughter at the RCN conference in Bournemouth[215]. Earlier in the same week she had been listened to with quiet contempt by Unison at their national conference. She also had a difficult passage with changes to the training programmes of junior doctors and the Medical Training Application Service [MTAS] and she was forced to make a public apology for its shortcomings. She criticised GPs for taking money as income when it was intended for investment

---

[214] A plan to close seven community hospitals in Gloucestershire was blocked by Ministers.
[215] John Carvel. Guardian 27/4/06

in their practices. Norman Warner one of her ministerial team forced a sharp cut back in an unaffordable PFI programme including high profile schemes like the Paddington Basin in London. He had also led on a reduction in the number of Primary Care Trusts and plans for the removal of their community services organisations which created a lot of controversy when community nursing staff feared losing their jobs. It was quietly dropped. There was a Health Industry Task Force designed to stimulate the medical device and other health industries.

In May 2007 Hewitt survived a vote of no confidence in the Commons after a debate about the application system for medical training. She was, Andrew Lansley said, guilty of serial incompetence and a failure to listen to advice.

Although personable at a one to one level she was not popular with civil servants whose numbers were being sharply reduced. In October 2006 only 37% of workers at the Department of Health were confident in the leadership she provided. When ministers went on visits, she insisted that they met staff without their managers present.

She led strongly on the ban on smoking in public places in the teeth of fierce opposition which included her predecessor John Reid who argued for an exemption for private clubs and pubs that did not serve food. The complete ban came into force on 1st July 2007. It was, said Liam Donaldson the CMO, "a momentous move". She tried to secure a tax increase on alcopops, but this was blocked.

Throughout her term of office her commitment to the NHS was evident and decidedly left wing. The NHS was there when you needed it and was free to all at the point of need. She did not approve of top up payments as a way of raising new money as this would conflict with equity. "The UK needed to keep the ethos and values of the NHS whilst transforming the way it worked in order to match patient expectations in a consumer society."

She was not reappointed when Gordon Brown became Prime Minister in June 2007 and instead took on several controversial consultancies in health-related organisations. She left Parliament in 2010 but not before joining Geoff Hoon in a leadership challenge to Gordon Brown. She was drawn into a cash for access scandal in 2010 and for a time was suspended from the Parliamentary Labour

Party. In the end the Party decided to take no further action against her. She was appointed Chair of the NHS Sustainability and Transformation Board for Norfolk in 2017.

She had a turbulent two years as Health Secretary partly because of her own style but also because she confronted and dealt with two major issues; smoking and overspending. It was she said the toughest two years of her life but also the most rewarding. Her strategic vision was swallowed up in the financial crisis but some of her team's ideas were to re-emerge under Alan Johnson and Ara Darzi.

She was a competent minister in difficult times and knew instinctively that even in hard times you had to keep building visions about the future.

1948-Date

ALAN JOHNSON

June 2007-June 2009

Labour

Alan Johnson was born in London. He left school at fifteen to stack shelves at Tesco and later became a postman. He joined the Labour Party in 1971 with distinctly left-wing views. He became a full-time union official from 1987 and five years later General Secretary of the Union of Communication Workers.

He entered Parliament in 1997 as MP for Hull West and Hessle and immediately took up junior ministerial posts. He entered the cabinet in 2004 as Secretary of State for Work and Pensions and then in 2005 Trade and Industry.

He came to Health in 2007 in Gordon Brown's first cabinet. He found an NHS still absorbing the Milburn reforms, but Patricia Hewitt had largely but painfully sorted out the worst of the overspending problems in the NHS.

Johnson had little enthusiasm for the internal market and scrapped the independent treatment centres. He wanted a period of relative stability whilst ministers worked out what to do next. There were to be no more national targets until the way forward was clear. A World Class Commissioning initiative was launched by Mark Britnell.[216] It brought ambition and excitement to the commissioning process but according to the House of Commons Select Committee it failed to achieve its own ambitious targets.

Ara Darzi a London surgeon had joined Johnson's team with a seat in the Lords and embarked upon his Next Stage Review of the NHS. Darzi a London surgeon had just completed a review of the NHS in London which had been well received by the government. Darzi thought that the NHS was two thirds along the modernisation path set by Milburn's Hospital Plan in 2000. He and David Nicholson the NHS Chief Executive toured the country seeking views about next steps. An interim report came out in October 2007 and a final report in June 2008. It reinforced developing policy ideas about improving quality in the NHS. The NHS needed to move from a centrally driven target-based service to one in which local decision making was empowered and funding was based on both activity and clinical outcomes. Services needed to be joined up better, made more accessible and be better integrated. A National Quality Board would be formed. Patients' rights would be consolidated into a new NHS Constitution and personalised health budgets would be trialled. Primary care would be expanded and increasingly based in polyclinics; GP payment systems would provide incentives for maintaining health as well as providing care. The Care Quality Commission would be given more enforcement powers. Social enterprises run by NHS staff would be encouraged as would combined health and social care organisations.[217] Each Region produced an action plan to implement the Darzi proposals.

The report was well received although some thought it to be "neutered radicalism" designed to reassure the clinical staff of the future of the NHS and their role in it as leaders.[218] One can detect the hand of David Nicholson in both his interim and final reports. What will be particularly remembered is the Darzi call for action on quality.

---

[216] Britnell resigned in 2009 to join KPMG and became head of their world-wide health practice.
[217] Darzi resigned in July 2009 to return to clinical practice.
[218] Norman Warner. A suitable case for treatment. Grosvenor House publishing 2011.

Alongside the Darzi implementation was work in the field of public health stimulated by another Wanless Report. He had reported good progress in smoking reduction but little progress on the organisation and delivery of public health policies.[219] There was also an internal review to examine the evidence that cancer survival results in the UK were not as good as those in other countries.

Johnson got into some difficulty with a patient who wanted to buy Avastin a drug which was not available to NHS patients. Johnson told Parliament "that patients cannot in one episode of treatment be treated by the NHS and then allowed as part of the same episode of treatment pay money for more drugs. That way, he said, lies the end of the founding principles of the NHS".[220]

He intervened when the Maidstone Trust which had been struggling with high infection rates tried to part company with its Chief Executive. [221] He blocked the agreed severance payment, but his decision was later overturned by the Court of Appeal.

He would have been involved in the first thoughts about the handling of the swine flu epidemic.

In 2008 he published a three-year plan for improving services for people with a learning disability.

He was a popular minister in government. When he moved between the great Departments of State, he took a team of three civil servants [Press, Diary, and Secretary] and three political advisors with him. All briefs to the Prime Minister went through his political advisors. He believed in a permanent and apolitical civil service. If ministers were clear about what they wanted the civil service would do its utmost to deliver. He appointed the first part-time Permanent Secretary.[222]

---

[219] Wanless Report. Kings Fund 2007.
[220] In 2010 the Government created a Cancer Drugs Fund for drugs that had not yet been thoroughly appraised by NICE,
[221] His decision was later overturned by the Courts.
[222] Great Offices of State Lecture. November 2013.

His term in health was relatively quiet as the government worked its way through next steps. He took few initiatives himself. It all seemed to happen around him although letting it happen was a rare skill for a Secretary of State. In June 2009 he moved to the Home Office where one of his first acts was to sack the Chairman of the Advisory Committee on the misuse of drugs after a row about the classification of Ecstasy and Cannabis

He resigned from his post as shadow Chancellor of the Exchequer in 2011 for personal reasons but remained a backbench member of Parliament until 2017 when did not stand in the general election.

1950-Date.

ANDY BURNHAM

June 2009- May 2010

Labour

Andrew Burnham was born in Liverpool and went onto complete a degree in English at Cambridge. He joined the Labour Party at an early age and became a researcher for Tessa Jowell. After the general election in 1997 he worked briefly for the NHS Confederation before becoming a political advisor to Chris Smith then Secretary of State for Culture, Media and Sport.

He entered Parliament at the 2001 general election as MP for Leigh in Lancashire. His first senior ministerial post was Minister of State [Health] under Patricia Hewitt in May 2006. He had the ministerial lead first on quality and professional regulation in the wake of the Shipman inquiry and then on financial recovery. On the advice of officials, he had approved the application for Foundation status by Mid Staffordshire NHS Trust for submission to Monitor.

He became Chief Secretary to the Treasury in Gordon Brown's first Cabinet in 2007.

He became Secretary of State for Health in 2009 but was only in post for twelve months. Top of his in tray on appointment was the aftermath of the Healthcare Commission report on Stafford Hospital. He found to his surprise that the hospital still had no permanent replacement for the Chair and Chief Executive. He demanded action but that fell to Monitor rather than the Department of Health. David Nicholson the Chief Executive made some proposals which were quickly implemented but dressed up as Monitor's decisions. In the face of mounting public anger there was no place for constitutional niceties. He later explained that whilst ministers should stay away from the direct management of the NHS as far as was possible politicians had to retain an override power when public safety or poor governance was evident.

Burnham authorised the first Stafford Inquiry in July 2009[223]. The Inquiry was led by a lawyer Robert Francis but controversially it was not a public inquiry. It reported in February 2010 with its awful patient stories and led to press speculation about 1000's of deaths[224] The second Stafford Inquiry set up by Lansley, again chaired by Robert Francis, was a public inquiry into the actions of the wider NHS including the Department of Health. Burnham was heavily criticised by patient groups at this Inquiry, to which he gave evidence under oath, for not taking their concerns seriously enough when in office. He strongly denied this. [225]

The Care Quality Commission had begun to operate on 1st April 2009 and so Burnham was involved in the direction of its early work and the search for effective quality measures. He picked up the ongoing work flowing from the Darzi review including personal health budgets which he described as the "ultimate expression of power and influence being handed to patients". Swine Flu was also a major problem during his term of office. The CMO had advised him of the possibility of 65,000 deaths. The prearranged contingency plans

---

[223] The Francis Inquiries. Brian Edwards. Kindle.
[224] The second Francis Inquiry into the wider NHS was set up by Andrew Lansley as a public Inquiry in June 2010.
[225] He gave evidence on 6th September 2011.

were launched at considerable cost. The death rate turned out to be far lower than predicted but a later review confirmed that the decision to launch the contingency plan had been the correct one in the circumstances.

In 2010 he entered the Labour leadership contest but finished fourth with less than 10% of the vote. In 2011 he became shadow Secretary of State for Health and spearheaded the opposition to the Lansley reforms. His mission he claimed was to keep the NHS true to its Bevanite roots and stop the privatisation of the NHS. His plans, at least while in opposition, would merge health and social service budgets and give patients the right to access their clinical records on line.

He never really had time to make an impact as Secretary of State for Health. In opposition he was to lead the fight against the Lansley reforms. He later became Mayor of Greater Manchester which chosen to pilot a devolved NHS.

1970-date

ANDREW LANSLEY

May 2010-September 2012

Conservative

Andrew Lansley was born in Essex and educated at Exeter University. He became President of the Guild of Students as a broad left candidate. His father was a distinguished medical laboratory scientist. His first wife was a GP. His second wife Sally was a major player in the communications company Low which was very active in Europe.

Before entering politics, Lansley was a civil servant and at one point in this career was private secretary to Norman Tebbitt. He left the civil service to become Director of the British Chambers of Commerce and in 1990 he was appointed to run the Conservative Research Department. His team included David Cameron and George Osborne. In 1997 he was elected MP for South Cambridgeshire. In 2004 Lansley became shadow Secretary of State for Health in the shadow Cabinet of Michael Howard. He retained this post until he took over the substantive job in May 2010 under David Cameron and his coalition government. He was to hold the health brief for a total of eight years and regarded himself as an expert in the field. Health was, he told his colleagues, the only ministerial job he had ever wanted. He was very difficult to argue with and once his mind was clear on an issue very difficult to shift. He had been planning what to do when he came into office for some years and had draft white papers and bills ready for an immediate start. The Tory manifesto for the 2010 general election included the creation of a national NHS Board to allocate resources and provide guide lines for GPs who would become the commissioners of health care. Patients would be able to choose any provider in either the public or the private sector provided they met NHS quality standards and prices. The power of Ministers to get involved in the day to day affairs of the NHS would be limited. In their manifesto the Liberal Democrats [now part of the coalition] had called for the removal of Strategic Health Authorities and closer links with local government. They had poured scorn on the idea of an independent NHS Commissioning Board. Both parties had agreed to stick with the principle of a service free to all at the point of need.

Lansley found himself in a coalition government. He had Paul Burstow a Liberal Democrat as one of his two Ministers of State. Simon Burns was the other. Compromises had to be found.

The initial Coalition agreement said almost nothing about the NHS[226] but the final agreement when it eventually emerged set out almost all of Lansley's plans including the creation of an NHS Board, GP commissioning and the right of patients to choose any qualified provider. The coalition also committed themselves to increased investment in the NHS. The Liberal Democrats secured directly elected members on the Boards of Primary Care Trusts which at this stage were to remain in place, despite a promise of a 25% cut in

---

[226] May 2010.

administration. It was, Cameron and his deputy Clegg, announced a blending of Conservative and Liberal Democrat ideas.

Two months later Lansley published his white paper *Equity and Excellence: Liberating the NHS*[227].

There would indeed be a new independent NHS Commissioning Board at a national level, NHS England as it would eventually be called. It would be lean and expert and take the politics and the politicians out of the day to day management of the NHS.

The Department of Health would exert what control it needed via a mandate renewed every few years. All NHS Trusts would move into Foundation status with their freedoms increased. Ministers would no longer be able to meddle in hospital affairs. New and independent providers would have a right to supply treatment and services to NHS patients if they met NHS quality standards and were within NHS costs ["any qualified provider"]. Budgets would be passed to GPs to manage because they understood what their patients needed. They, Lansley argued, would become active, intelligent and patient sensitive commissioners. A new economic regulator would be created [Monitor] to oversee the Foundation Trusts. Health Watch a new organisation would speak for the consumers. The Care Quality Commission would inspect quality. Public Health would transfer to Local Government. New Health and Well Being Boards would join up health and social care planning. GP commissioning would be compulsory for general practitioners [not by practice but by 211 larger groupings of practices].

This compulsion would turn out to be a critical decision and was made in the days running up to the publication of the White paper. As GPs took up the rein of commissioning with NHS England the 152 Primary Care Trusts would no longer be required. Once Strategic Health Authorities lost oversight of both commissioning and the Foundation Trusts they too could go. There would be a 45% reduction in NHS management costs and further cuts at the Department of Health and its arm's length bodies. A massive shakeout was in prospect. David Nicholson then Chief Executive of the whole NHS described the reforms as "so big you could see them from space".

---

[227] Cmd 7881.July 2010.

It came as a bombshell to an NHS who had been told during the election campaign that there would be no more "pointless and disruptive" top down reorganisations.

Although people were shocked by the scale of the planned changes they should not have been surprised. Most had been trailed by Lansley whilst he was in opposition.[228] Lansley was not helped by *friends* in the private sector like Kingsley Manning talking about the denationalisation of health services and the biggest transfer of employment out of the public sector since the days of Margaret Thatcher. This was not a wholesale privatisation although Lansley did keep quite close to a range of private sector providers.

The opposition had five principal targets; privatisation, the scale and cost of the reorganisation, the weakening of the Secretary of State's overall responsibility for the NHS, the competency of general practice to commission services and the impact their rationing role would have on their relationship with their patients. There was another rather understated concern as to whether general practice could handle the inevitable conflicts of interest inherent in combining the roles of commissioner and provider. The doctor's leaders and many others believed it could all have been achieved if GP's had simply assumed a larger role on Primary Care Trusts. The House of Commons Library confirmed that almost all the key reforms could be achieved under current legislation.[229] But Lansley, rather like Ken Clarke some years earlier, wanted radical change that could not default back. He wanted the changes nailed in with legislation.

What the reforms lacked was a clear narrative that could be understood by the public and the staff of the NHS. Few really understood that the NHS was moving from a managed national service to a regulated industry rather like the telecommunications, water or energy sectors. Some warned that in its new form the NHS would be open to the stringencies of EU competition law. David Nicholson moved quickly to strengthen national controls over the NHS "whilst we build the new system".

---

[228] See Nick Timmins Never Again. The story of the Health and Social Care Act 2012.Kings Fund. London
[229] Andy Burnham had sought this opinion. Stephen Dorrell also argued this point.

In October 2010 the formal consultation on the plan closed with a wave of scepticism and anger. David Cameron became alarmed and asked Oliver Letwin [Conservative] and Danny Alexander [Liberal Democrat] to review matters. They reported back that the plans were fine if the transition could be handled well. To his surprise David Nicholson was asked to stay on as Chief Executive and become Chief Executive designate of NHS England to oversee the changes. There would no longer be a Chief Executive of the NHS as a whole. The Roy Griffiths concept had lasted only 25 years. Lansley invited Alan Milburn to become chairman of NHS England, but he declined.

The Bill, when published in January 2011, was 550 pages long with 280 clauses and 22 schedules. Changing the relationship between ministers and the NHS was a complex business. As the Bill progressed through Parliament the debate became polarised and increasingly angry. The BMA and others objected strongly to almost everything in the Bill. At the end of March Prime Minister Cameron and Clegg decided to defuse the row by enforcing *a pause* in the Parliamentary process whilst further consultations took place. Clegg accused Lansley of putting the ideological cart before the political horse. Lansley was visibly upset but chose not to resign. The RCN booed him at their conference and delegates backed a motion of no confidence. Dr Steve Field a GP was asked to chair a Forum of interested parties to look at the reform package.[230,231] The Forum had 56 members drawn from a wide range of interested parties and over 3000 people attended their listening events. Their first report appeared in June 2011 and a second report in January 2012. As well as talking to leading players in the NHS Field had what he described as extraordinary access to the Prime Minister during the Forum's work.[232]

Once the Forum conclusions had been digested GP Consortia had been replaced by Clinical Commissioning Groups with an accountable officer. Monitor would be charged with promoting integrated care and his responsibility to promote competition softened. Clinical senates would provide a voice for specialists. The Secretary of State would remain ultimately accountable for the NHS.

---

[230] The invitation came from Simon Burns the Minister of State.
[231] A former President of the Royal College of General Practice
[232] Evidence to Health Select Committee 16/6/2011.

The BMA called the changes "a respray" but nevertheless the Bill completed its passage through the Commons in early September and went back to the Lords where the fight continued under the leadership of Shirley Williams a social democrat[233]. Some leading Liberal Democrats argued that the Bill was an attempt to curtail or end the State's role in the provision of public services.[234] The Presidents of the Royal Medical Colleges voiced their opposition. The BMA called for Lansley's resignation. It was quite difficult to identify many people who supported the Bill. In the House of Lords amendment followed amendment as Lansley slowly gave ground. The removal of the cap on the amount of private work undertaken by NHS Foundation Trusts had been replaced by a cap of 49% of income and then further controlled with a requirement that any increase over 5% would need the consent of the Trust's Governors. The Bill finally cleared the Lords with 2000 amendments. Royal Assent was given on 27th March 2012. Although Lansley's original plan had been badly mauled its key elements remained in place.

Behind the scenes David Nicholson and the Department of Health had been quietly preparing the ground for swift implementation. In the NHS staff began to hunt for new jobs in those parts of the administrative structure that would remain. They left behind unfinished much good work in the efficiency and quality fields.

The Department of Health had also been preoccupied by the second Mid Staffordshire Public Inquiry which had started taking evidence in public at the end of 2010. Lansley and Cameron had agreed to a public inquiry whilst in opposition. The Department expressed their doubts about the wisdom of this arguing that the problems in Stafford were now clear and what was needed was firm corrective action rather than a lengthy and expensive inquiry. As the Inquiry rolled on the patient stories of neglect captured the headlines along with speculation about the number of avoidable deaths that had occurred.[235] During the second part of the Inquiry which focused on the role of government and public authorities Una O'Brien the Permanent Secretary, David Nicholson, Andy Burnham the former Secretary of State and a raft of senior officials from both the Department of Health and the NHS all found themselves giving

---

[233] She eventually relented as the Government gave ground.
[234] John Pugh, Chair of the Liberal Democrat's Health Committee.
[235] The newspapers put the number at over a 1000. The truth was nobody knew for certain.

evidence under oath[236]. The Department found itself having to release reams of sometimes embarrassing inhouse papers and emails. The final report would be presented to Lansley's predecessor in February 2013 with its demands for a change in the culture of the NHS.[237]

Another scandal that needed managing resulted from a Panorama programme about abuse at a private care home at Winterbourne View in Gloucestershire. Norman Lamb the Liberal Democrat minister led the coalition response.

One of the ideas that survived the coalition agreement was that of creating a Cancer Drugs Fund which allowed patients in England to access drugs that had not been approved by NICE on economic grounds. It started in 2011 and was updated in 2016. The policy was not universally popular. The Financial Times attacked the fund as a populist measure that represented poor value for money and undermined NICE. The Public Accounts Committee agreed with this judgement. The budget for 2017/18 was £340m.

Lansley had got his Bill through Parliament, but his reputation had been badly damaged in the process. In a Cabinet reshuffle in September 2012 David Cameron moved him to the post of Leader of the House of Commons and Jeremy Hunt took over as Secretary of State for Health.

Lansley has emerged as a complex character who fought through Parliament a major reform of the NHS. His big mistake was the failure to express a coherent vision of the future of the NHS from the start although he himself had a very detailed understanding of the changes he proposed. Some commentators think that this may have been a deliberate attempt to hide the scale of the plans as they were driven through Parliament. More likely is that the plans were not perfectly formed at the start and evolved over time. Lansley was not an effective communicator and at times could not understand why people could not comprehend what to him was obvious or self-evident. Despite his plan to empower doctors to control NHS investment Lansley secured few friends in the clinical community. Their attitudes were no doubt coloured by the impeding financial storm which was beginning to impact on the NHS front line. The NHS had been promised protection from the worst aspects of the economic downturn but in practice this meant operating with little if any

---

[236] For a Day by Day account of the Inquiry see The Stafford Story. Edwards. Amazon Kindle. 2013.

growth and securing massive efficiency savings [£20 billion by 2015] for reinvestment. [238]

After an uncertain start he worked well with David Nicholson and the civil service. Although he hoped that his reforms would be hard wired into the core of the NHS many judged that they were just a staging post to an even more uncertain future. Some Clinical Commissioning Groups would invigorate commissioning, but others would not, and more reorganisations were forecast. In secondary care the need to rationalise the hospital sector was becoming clearer day by day, but Lansley's reorganisation made system wide change even more difficult than it had been before.

Judgements about Lansley's term of office have to be essentially negative. His policy ideas were not all that far removed from the direction set by Alan Milburn and should not have generated the controversy they did. Limiting politicians' ability to meddle in NHS operational affairs should have been an easy sell for those inside the NHS. Putting doctors in charge of commissioning should also have been easy. The trouble was that he saw the way forward in terms of parliamentary process rather than explaining his plans and ideas to all the interested parties and building up support. He moved too quickly and did not spend enough time preparing for the economic storm that was on the way and clouded much of the debate about his reforms. If the NHS Forum had met at the start of the process rather than during a crisis towards the end implementation might have been much easier. Chris Ham from the Kings Fund was less forgiving. " People from the NHS focused on rearranging the deck chairs rather than the core business of improving health care". All the other things Lansley did or initiated whilst in office [including the response to the H1N1 pandemic, which was highly commended by WHO], are all lost in the wake of the reform controversy. Nigel Edwards was later to refer to the Lansley reforms as one of the greatest policy failures of the century.[239]

He stood down as an MP in 2015 and was awarded a life peerage as Baron Lansley of Orwell in Cambridgeshire.

1956-Date.

---

[238] The 2010 Spending review provided the NHS with real terms growth of 0.1%.
[239] Nuffield Trust Newsletter 2019

JEREMY.R. S. HUNT

September 2012- July 2018

Conservative

Jeremy Hunt was born in Kensington, London. He was the elder son of Admiral Sir Nicholas Hunt. He was educated at Charterhouse and Oxford where he graduated with a first in PPE. David Cameron and Boris Johnson were contemporaries.

After university he worked as a management consultant and an English language teacher in Japan. He married Lucia Guo who was born in China. On his return to the UK he worked in Public Relations and Directory publishing.

He entered Parliament in 2005 having won Virginia Bottomley's old seat in South West Surrey. He had shadow roles in Disabled People and Culture, Media and Sport.

In the Coalition government he became Culture Secretary and had to deal with issues such as the Murdoch Empire and BskyB, the Levison Inquiry into the Press and preparations for the Olympic games.

In September 2012 he became Secretary of State for Health. It was he said, "a huge task and the biggest privilege of his life".

His brief from David Cameron was implement the Lansley reforms as quietly as possible, keep talking about services and quality and look after David Nicholson.[240]

Hunt became the patient's friend as scandals about community care emerged alongside the horror stories from the Stafford Inquiry which had demanded a change in the culture of the NHS. He did defend David Nicholson under heavy attack from all sides for the events in Stafford on condition that he said nothing to the press. He beefed up the Care Quality Commission and told Monitor and the Trust Development Authority to develop intervention strategies for use when things went seriously wrong. He tripled Monitors budget and charged CQC with developing an Ofsted type of rating system for all NHS services. Bruce Keogh the Medical Director of NHS England was sent round the country reviewing those hospitals with very high hospital standardised mortality ratios. Hunt made it clear that quality must always be more important than cost which led to a sharp increase in nursing staff numbers. It also laid the seeds of the financial crisis that would follow as financial deficits grew. Breaching a cash limit was no longer a sackable offence. A serious quality failure was. Hunt thought he could balance overall NHS expenditure at the top and most years this worked.

Competition was still part of a conservative NHS. Hunt had previously co-authored a book calling for the NHS "to be replaced by a new system of health provision in which people would pay money into personal health accounts which would enable them to shop around for care or treatment from public or private providers". Those who could not afford to pay enough would be supported by the State. However private sector organisations told him how difficult it was to break into the CCG commissioning world. Hunt did little in practical terms to ease the pathway for private providers. Circle a private company had taken on the management of Hitchingbrook Hospital from the NHS in 2010 with the approval of Andrew Lansley but withdrew from its contract in 2015 claiming it was no longer financially sustainable.[241] The Competition Commission stopped a planned merger in Dorset[242] claiming it would reduce choice. Competition law was increasingly a problem. Hunt did support NHS England's plans to expand personal health budgets for patients.

Hunt had a distinctive style of working which was to select a limited number of objectives and pursue them persistently over time. His initial four were better

---

[240] Nick Timmins .Five Giants. A Biography of the Welfare State. Harper Collins 1995.
[241] It remains open as an NHS organisation following a merger with a larger Trust in 2017.
[242] Portsmouth and Poole.

survival rates for killer diseases such as cancer; ensuring care was as important as treatment; improving care for people with long term conditions and particularly those with dementia. These four later grew to include amongst other things mental health and emergency care. Every Monday morning everybody involved was called to his office to review progress. This was not the distance Lansley had in mind. In the absence of an NHS Chief Executive somebody had to hold the now fragmented NHS together and Hunt saw this as his role at least in as far as his priorities were concerned. The absence of a system leader strengthened his grip on the NHS rather than weakened it. Eventually Nicholson and Bennett [the man from Monitor who regulated Foundation trusts] began to find reasons to miss these Monday meetings and sent subordinates instead. The Monday morning teleconference became commonplace.

NHS England had been set up with David Nicholson as Chief Executive in April 2011 first as a Special Health Authority and later as a Non-Departmental Public Body operating under a mandate agreed with the Department of Health. It was based in Leeds rather like its predecessor NHS Executive to create or give the impression of independence from Ministers in London. Like most other public bodies, it met in public and published its papers. The annual review of the mandate was sometimes a fraught occasion with Malcolm Grant the Chair of NHS England complaining in 2013 that the latest draft represented a move back to "command and control". In practice Hunt overrode the mandate whenever he wanted to. He was after all the Secretary of State.

He personally reviewed all the plans for handling the forecast winter emergencies. He accepted the need for a 24hour, seven days a week NHS. He was heavily criticised for this by the Public Accounts Committee. He had approved a plan that was in their view incoherent and uncosted. His allegation that NHS hospitals were unsafe at a weekend was rejected by Fiona Goodlee the editor of the BMJ who accused him of misrepresenting the evidence. A leaked internal report from within the Department reported that no evidence could be found to link increased consultant numbers to reduced weekend mortality or reduced lengths of hospital stay.

He called in Chief Executives of CCG's who were innovating with new services or in trouble. He issued standards on hospital food and guidance on charges for hospital car parking. He kept a board with breaches of "never events "in his office. He was very much in touch with the front line of the NHS often, but not always, with media present. It was Ministers who created a Better Care Fund [£2Billion] to stimulate integrated care. In December 2015 NHS England charged every locality to produce five-year sustainability and transformation plans. Some areas recruited former secretaries of State including Hewitt and Dorrell to chair their transformation boards. Many of the plans generated by these boards included changes to the acute sector and bed reductions which rang alarm bells for ministers. NHS England was told to be careful.

Hunt's concern for quality, and headlines about a junior doctor who was struck off after admitting an error of clinical judgement, led him to take steps towards a learning rather than a blame culture when clinical accidents or mistakes occurred.

He imposed a new contract on junior doctors in 2016 after a four year and eventually fruitless battle with the BMA. The conflict was eventually settled after much behind the scenes talks. Both sides claimed victory.

He increased the number of student places in medical schools by 1500 and announced that the NHS would be self-sufficient for doctors by 2025.Sceptics doubted the growth he had agreed to would achieve this objective. The gender balance in medicine was continuing to widen and those entering general practice were increasingly opting for part-time salaried contracts.

His frustration with independent NHS organisations was at times shared by the people in Downing Street who struggled to get their way on the introduction of the "Friends and family test" as a means of judging NHS organisations. Jane Ellison the Minister for Public Health was reported in the Observer telling a private Tory meeting "I don't know how much many of you realise that with the Lansley Act we pretty much gave away control of the NHS"[243]

David Nicholson decided to retire in April 2014.He had implemented the Lansley reforms but the independence that was at their heart was still missing and he had had a hard time with the Stafford Inquiry. His successor was Simon Stevens a former advisor to Labour ministers. In October 2014 Stevens

---

[243] The Observer 2014

published the NHS England Five Year Plan which was well received. Stevens clearly preferred choice to competition. He and Dave Bennett the Chief Executive of Monitor named the sum the NHS needed to survive and grow [£8 Billion]. Negotiations with Treasury had in the past always been the role of the Secretary of State. Hunt had seen the plan only 48 hours before its publication although there had always been back channels with the Department and the Treasury during its preparation. In the end the Government found the money although some critics accused the Treasury of overstating the scale of the investment. It was more catch up money.

Hunt for his part acknowledged that the market would never be able to deliver satisfactorily integrated care. He was still heavily engaged in the short-term problems of emergency care with a cabinet committee no less trying to sort out the problems in social care because of the impact it was having on hospital admissions. He asked Dr Nigel Watson, a leading GP to review the GP Partnership model which was under significant threat as more and more GPs opted for the salaried option. He established a Public Inquiry into the use of contaminated blood products during the 1970s and 1980s.[244]

Like some of his predecessors he was attracted to a high-tech future fuelled by Artificial Intelligence. The dream was fine, but the long-term implementation plan and earmarked funding was invisible. It was a baton his predecessor would pick up. Progress would be littered with practical problems stemming mainly from the independence of NHS trusts. Some of these difficulties had been highlighted in May 2017 by a cyber-attack on the NHS which had affected a third of all trusts and many general practices.

Towards the end of his term in office he supported NHS England in a move towards Accountable Care Organisations which brought together all the NHS organisations in a defined geographical area to develop integrated care. A competitive market was unlikely to deliver sustainable models of integrated care. By now the Departmental brief had swung firmly in the direction of community care. Departmental priorities included "transform primary, community and social care to keep people living more independent, healthier lives for longer in the communities."

---

[244] Announced by the Prime Minister in July 2017.

In 2018 he declined to accept a change of office in a cabinet reshuffle and instead added the highly charged issue of social care to his ministerial brief. He then became Secretary of State for Health and Social Welfare. Within Whitehall this made little difference except that Hunt was now in charge of preparations for a green paper on the future of social care and who should pay for it. He led the pressure on Downing Street for increased investment in both health and social welfare and won a major investment of £20 billion over five years [3.4%] It was keyed to a long-term investment plan to be agreed with NHS England. It was very good news but only enough to stabilise the current system which by the middle of 2018 was reporting an underlying deficit of £4.3b and growing. The arguments about long term funding remained as did the difficult policy decisions on funding social care which he would leave to his successor. The argument with the Treasury did expose some of his thinking about longer term funding. He judged that the community would pay more for their NHS if asked and he toyed seriously with the notion of a ring-fenced national insurance system. The Treasury had always resisted the idea of hypothecated funding for the NHS and seemed unlikely to change their position.

In July 2018 Hunt left the Department of Health to become Foreign Secretary following the resignation of Boris Johnson.

He was in post longer than any of his predecessors [almost six years]. He got on well with his civil servants. Occasionally he bucked the system by, for example, talking directly to patients with complaints. On a one to one basis he won the respect of many NHS professionals. His public image was generally one of measured judgement and compassion. He abandoned NHS targets if he judged them to be unrealistic or unhelpful. He led the NHS through a long period of austerity with growth rates during his term of office averaging around 1.3 %. The inevitable battles with the BMA never got out of control although he took a lot of abuse in the media. He did get the grudging respect of the BMA for the financial settlement he secured in his last months in office. He gave NHS England a lot of space although not as much as Lansley might have wished. He never rubbished in public his predecessor and was a loyal member of the May cabinet. He often talked about the benefits of a National Health Service with conviction.

He achieved a lot during his period of office perhaps more than he received the credit for. He was one of the better Secretaries of State.

He was succeeded by Matt Hancock.

1966-Date

What makes a good Minister of Health.

What makes a good Minister of Health? Robert Maxwell, a former Director of the Kings Fund, addressed this question in 1981[245] and concluded that four characteristics marked a successful tenure. Time in post, strategic vision and commitment, good judgement about priorities and leadership. Thirty years later the judgemental framework can shift a little to include communication skills both within the NHS and with the public.

The political and economic context in which individuals found themselves is all important. The greatest test of political leadership is often found during hard times rather than in days of growth and expansion.

If the principal measure is what they achieved, then four ministers [perhaps six] stand out. Bevan for having the strength and the vision to create the NHS in the first place, Powell for rebuilding it in the 1960's and starting to reshaping mental health, Clarke for injecting life and energy into the management of a growing service and

---

[245] The Lancet.27th June 1981.

Milburn for a massive reinvestment programme from 2000.[246] Bevan had the vision, Powell had the purpose, Clarke had the toughness to drive change and Milburn had the money. All had more than three years in post and two, Clarke and Milburn had quite long stints as Ministers of State in Health. Hunt could perhaps be added to this list for steering the NHS safely through a long period of austerity and giving NHS England space to develop. However, set against this must be weighed the financial deficits he left within the NHS. The final candidate could be Norman Fowler who brought general management into the NHS and led the public health campaign about Aids.

Others made their contribution in different ways. Macleod provided a period of calm whilst Bevan's plans bedded in. Walker-Smith did some of the groundwork that would lead to Enoch Powell's rebuilding programme. Kenneth Robinson revitalised general practice and took the first serious steps to reduce cigarette smoking. Crossman pushed for improvements in mental health, but his attention was focused on social security. Joseph worked hard, but his reputation is clouded by a failed reorganisation. Castle helped the nurses, but her term was mired in political conflict. David Ennals was liked and respected by the health professions but was inhibited by the ongoing work of the Royal Commission. Jenkin confronted the Trade Unions but could not resist yet another reorganisation. Waldegrave tightened the focus on health outcomes and Bottomley softened the edges of the competitive market and developed thinking about quality. Dorrell created a policy framework for Dobson to build upon with some success in a Labour government. Hewitt resolved a testing financial crisis which could have been very dangerous indeed if it had not been sorted out. Reid did little, but

---

[246] It is too early to reach a judgement on the Lansley reforms.

Johnson energised commissioning and brought in Ari Darzi to chart a new future with David Nicholson. Lansley failed to explain his reforms and convince people that they would lead to a better NHS.

The best ministers have created an effective working relationship with their civil servants and built on work initiated by their predecessors. Norman Fowler and Ken Stowe his Permanent Secretary had six productive years together. Building a good working arrangement with the health professions was an effective means of making progress for some but those who made the most progress had to fight pitched battles with the BMA. Intelligent ministers listened to what the leaders of the professions had to say, respected their professionalism and ethics but expected them to be instinctively suspicious of politician led change. In the early years' ministers found Dr George Godber, CMO, a great source of advice and support.

Many ministers resorted to organisational change and some did so having promised not to. It rarely worked but they would have left office before this became obvious. They all proved very expensive, shed many experienced managers and with them many of the quality and efficiency gains secured in earlier years.

Securing good financial settlements with the Treasury has been an important success measure for the NHS and some were better at it than others. Dobson, Milburn and Hunt secured by far the greatest increases in NHS funding.

By 2018 the degree of separation between ministers and the NHS was quite wide with Foundation Trusts and an arm's length NHS England. The principle lever Ministers have at their disposal is the framework agreement between the Department of Health and NHS England which is reviewed every three years. Without legislative change a Secretary of State can no longer act as defacto Chief Executive of the NHS. The Chair of a very large holding company would be a better comparator although this will not stop ministers intervening in day to day matters from time to time when the politics drive them. They remain accountable to Parliament for the NHS. The long-term funding for the NHS and social welfare is perhaps the toughest unresolved social policy issue facing this generation particularly as science is driving up cost. Ministers will continue to present their visions for the NHS in terms of reorganisation which is a substitute for not addressing what some would regard as the impossible political questions. However, whilst ever the NHS is funded from public sources political leadership will be inevitable and the NHS will continue to dominate the work of Secretaries of State for Health.

Based on this review the following points might be of help for future ministers.

- 5-year plans need to be part of a longer term vision. Sometimes ministers must sort out today before they can move forward to tomorrow. Long standing financial deficits are one serious blockage to progress in 2018. The moral hazard of resolving the problems at the expense of those who were responsible and prudent must be addressed.
- Visions that challenge the fundamental principles of the NHS are full of political hazard. Ministers who want to pursue this sort of change need clarity about their ideas and first-class communications. People from many persuasions will need to recognise their value and the need for change. They will be stronger if they have cross party consensus.

- Make the vision exciting to both the public and the health professions rather than challenging or negative. Targets only work if they are limited in number.
- Move with the grain of clinical practice. This is the core business of the NHS. Always distinguish between opinion and advice based on evidence. More integrated care is emerging as the clinical gold standard.
- Work with the health professions and listen to their views and ideas. Understand that they will always be suspicious of political change. They do represent vested interests but have been known to shift from negative positions.
- Resist plans for reorganisation unless you are sure it is vital. If people promise savings pre-commit them so they must be made. Ministers will always be confronted by the tension between a national service and local priority setting.
- Value the staff of the NHS. Rebuild the family spirit so they take a pride in their NHS. Build a learning culture and acknowledge mistakes.
- Value and respect the civil service. They rather like ministers with strong clear ideas who can face up to and resolve difficult issues.
- Be realistic about the speed of change. Avoid the temptation to pace reforms to match parliamentary timetables. Accept that you might have to pursue your predecessors' plans.
- Frankness and transparency are valued more than secrecy and duplicity.
- Putting the patient at the centre of NHS affairs needs to be more than a convenient slogan.
- Be prepared to trial new ideas before national implementation. Let the NHS innovate and be proud of its achievements.

Appendix 1

Ministers of Health

1.Aneurin BEVAN

Dates	Months in post	Age on Appointment	Party	Prime Minister
1945-1951	66	48	Labour	Clement Attlee

2. Hilary MARQUAND

Dates	Months in Post	Age	Party	Prime Minister
1951	10	50	Labour	Clement Attlee

3. Harry CROOKSHANK

Dates	Months in Post	Age	Party	Prime Minister
1951-1952	8	58	Conservative	Winston Churchill

4. Iain MACLEOD

Dates	Months in Post	Age	Party	Prime Minister
1952-1955	44	39	Conservative	Anthony Eden

5. Robin TURTON

Dates	Months in Post	Age	Party	Prime Minister
1955-1957	14	52	Conservative	Anthony Eden

6. Dennis VOSPER

Dates	Months in Post	Age	Party	Prime Minister
1957	8	41	Conservative	Harold Macmillan

7. Derek WALKER-SMITH

Dates	Months in Post	Age	Party	Prime Minister
1957-1960	35	47	Conservative	Harold Macmillan

8. Enoch POWELL

Dates	Months in Post	Age	Party	Prime Minister
1960-1963	40	48	Conservative	Harold Macmillan

9. Anthony BARBER

Dates	Months in Post	Age	Party	Prime Minister
1963-1964	13	43	Conservative	Alec Douglas-Home

10. Kenneth ROBINSON

Dates	Months in post	Age	Party	Prime Minister
1964-1968	49	53	Labour	Harold Wilson

Secretary of State for Social Services

11. Richard CROSSMAN

Dates	Months in Post	Age	Party	Prime Minister
1968-1970	20	61	Labour	Harold Wilson

12. Keith JOSEPH

Dates	Months in Post	Age	Party	Prime Minister
1970-1974	46	52	Conservative	Edward Heath

13 Barbara Castle

Dates	Months in post	Age	Party	Prime Minister
1974-1976	26	64	Labour	Harold Wilson

14. David ENNALS

Dates	Months in post	Age	Party	Prime Minister
1976-1979	38	54	Labour	James Callaghan

15. Patrick JENKIN

Dates	Months in post	Age	Party	Prime Minister
1979-1981	29	53	Conservative	Margaret Thatcher

16. Norman FOWLER

Dates	Months in post	Age	Party	Prime Minister
1981-1987	70	43	Conservative	Margaret Thatcher

17. John MOORE

Dates	Months in post	Age	Party	Prime Minister
1987-1988	13	50	Conservative	Margaret Thatcher

Secretary of State for Health

18. Kenneth CLARKE

Dates	Months in post	Age	Party	Prime Minister
1988-1990	29	48	Conservative	Margaret Thatcher

19. William WALDEGRAVE

Dates	Months in post	Age	Party	Prime Minister
1990-1992	18	44	Conservative	Margaret Thatcher

20. Virginia BOTTOMLEY

Dates	Months in post	Age	Party	Prime Minister
1992-1995	40	44	Conservative	Margaret Thatcher

21. Stephen DORRELL

Dates	Months in post	Age	Party	Prime Minister
1995-1997	23	43	Conservative	Margaret Thatcher

22. Frank DOBSON

Dates	Months in post	Age	Party	Prime Minister
1997-1999	30	57	Labour	Tony Blair

23. Alan MILBURN

Dates	Months in post	Age	Party	Prime Minister
1999-2003	45	46	Labour	Tony Blair

24. John REID

Dates	Months in post	Age	Party	Prime Minister
2003-2005	24	56	Labour	Tony Blair

25. Patricia HEWITT

Dates	Months in post	Age	Party	Prime Minister
2005-2007	26	57	Labour	Tony Blair

26. Alan JOHNSON

Dates	Months in post	Age	Party	Prime Minister
2007-2009	25	57	Labour	Gordon Brown

27. Andy BURNHAM

Dates	Months in post	Age	Party	Prime Minister
2009-2010	12	39	Labour	Gordon Brown

28. Andrew LANSLEY

Dates	Months in post	Age	Party	Prime Minister
2010-2012	29	54	Con/Lib Coalition	David Cameron

Secretary of State for Health and Social Care
[From 2018]

29. Jeremy HUNT

Dates	Months in post	Age	Party	Prime Minister
2012-2018	71	46	Conservative	David Cameron Theresa May

Printed in Great Britain
by Amazon